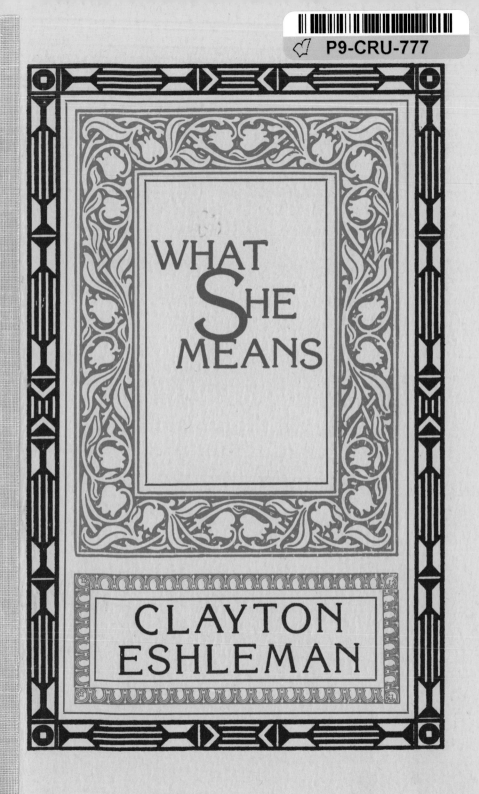

WHAT
SHE
MEANS

CLAYTON
ESHLEMAN

BY CLAYTON ESHLEMAN:

Mexico & North (1961)
Residence on Earth (translations of Pablo Neruda) (1962)
The Chavin Illumination (1965)
State of the Union (translations of Aimé Césaire, with
    Denis Kelly) (1966)
Lachrymae Mateo (1966)
Walks (1967)
Poemas Humanos/Human Poems (translations of César
    Vallejo) (1968)
Brother Stones (with William Paden's woodcuts) (1968)
Cantaloups & Splendor (1968)
T'ai (1969)
The House of Okumura (1969)
The House of Ibuki (1969)
Indiana (1969)
Yellow River Record (1969)
A Pitchblende (1969)
Bearings (1971)
Altars (1971)
A Caterpillar Anthology (editor & contributor) (1971)
The Sanjo Bridge (1972)
Coils (1973)
Human Wedding (1973)
Aux Morts (1974)
Spain, Take this Cup from Me (translations of Vallejo,
    with José Rubia Barcia) (1974)
Letter to André Breton (translation of Antonin Artaud)
    (1974)
Realignment (with drawings by Nora Jaffe) (1974)
Portrait of Francis Bacon (1975)
To Have Done with the Judgment of God
    (translation of Artaud, with Norman Glass) (1975)
The Gull Wall (1975)
Cogollo (1976)
Artaud the Mômo (translation of Artaud, with Norman
    Glass) (1976)
The Woman who Saw Through Paradise (1976)
Grotesca (1977)
On Mules sent from Chavin (1977)
Core Meander (1977)
The Gospel of Celine Arnaud (1977)
Battles in Spain (translations of Vallejo, with José Rubia
    Barcia) (1978)
The Name Encanyoned River (1978)

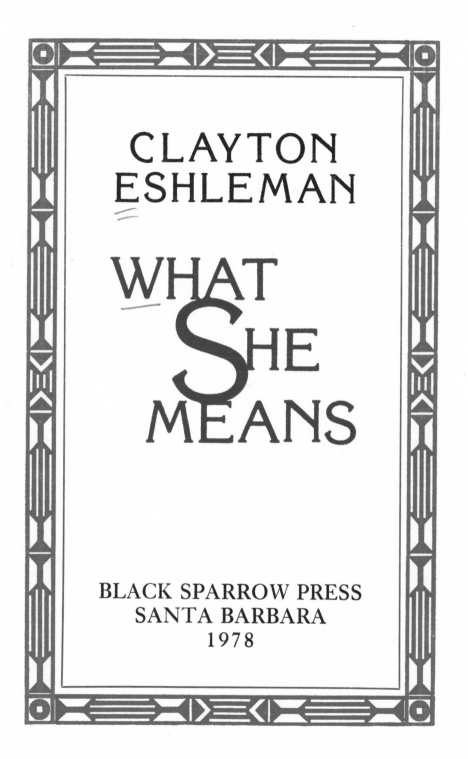

CLAYTON ESHLEMAN

WHAT SHE MEANS

BLACK SPARROW PRESS
SANTA BARBARA
1978

ACKNOWLEDGEMENTS

Some of these poems have appeared in: *Margins, New Directions Annual #33, American Poetry Review, Boundary 2, River Styx, Shell, Primer, The Spirit that Moves Us, Curtains* (England), *Bezoar, Text, Flute, Montemora, Pequod, New Wilderness Journal, Pearl* (Denmark), *California State Poetry Quarterly, Impact, Porch, Lettera* (Wales), *Tracks* and *Sarcophagus.* Early drafts for "For Milena Vodickova" appeared in *La Bas.* "The Woman who Saw Through Paradise" and "Alleluia Choruses" were printed under the title of the first poem as *Tansy 2.* "The Rancid Moonlight Hotel" was printed as a broadside for the poet's reading at The University of Connecticut Library, October 27, 1977. The poems written in Czechoslovakia appeared in a special issue of *Oasis* (England), #19, devoted to the author's poetry and translations. "The Name Encanyoned River" first appeared as a Treacle Press Book. Several of the poems first appeared in two books, *Cogollo* and *Grotesca* (England). "Chrysanthemum Lane" was printed as a post card by The Bellevue Press.

I would especially like to acknowledge the work my wife Caryl has done on the manuscript. All of the 65 poems have been talked through with her at every stage of their composition, and nearly all final drafts owe something to her editing.

LIBRARY OF CONGRESS CATALOGING IN PUBLICATION DATA

Eshleman, Clayton.
    What she means.

    I. Title.
PS3555.S5W5   811'.5'4   78-7502
ISBN 0-87685-347-5
ISBN 0-87685-346-7 pbk.

for Ira,

the absence of

the father and the son,

the name that never was,

" . . . the nothing that is."

Table of Contents

PREFACE

Caryl and I spent several months in southwestern France in 1974, looking at the painted and incised paleolithic caves. The thing that impressed me the most was the way that in some caves one animal or wandering line would be superimposed on others, in such a way that an ongoing net of figures, half-figures and non-figures was present, suggesting that in the minds of the drawers no fixed boundaries or center existed. In Les Combarelles, for example, the cave itself is a series of hairpin curves which are covered by thousands of intersecting forms and near-forms.

After we had seen the caves, Alexander Marshack showed us a photo of an incised ox-rib from an Acheulean dig near Bordeaux. The astonishing thing was, that at approximately 300,000 BC a hominid appears to have made a slash in the bone (referred to as a "core meander") and then to have placed his or her cutting instrument on the first slash and slashed to the side (creating what are referred to as "branch meanders"). In my opinion, whoever did this was creating history (thinking of it in the Olson-derived sense of "istorin," "to find out for oneself," in which I would stress "out," to find out, or exit, for the self).

Taking a lead from the caves and the terms used to describe ancient slash marks, I began, around 1975, to try to find a way to "meander" in my poetry, but also to keep a "core" at work within the meandering. It seems to me that the attempt to get rid of the "I" is as crippling as the attempt to get rid of the "other." Both are valid points of dynamic interchange and it is only when one is fixed and made central that the flux of contrariety is halted and opposites appear. In the poetry of *What She Means* I am seeking a focused movement forward, through material that remains open to lateral entry. As the focus proceeds, it is turned or meandered by what enters it from the side, thus filling and weighting the loom-like motion. I mean "focus," for what I am describing is not in any way "automatic writing," or that canard "free association." I use my poetry to think with, but want my thought to be open to its own spider alphabet, to twist, dissolve, whatever, out of my own experience, which means that background and childhood continue, as agents in composition, taking on different meanings, as opposed to disappearing, as I age.

The more I have worked in the way I describe, the more the "other" comes in, not only as that numinous presence about me in which I sense Caryl's multifoliate meaning, but other people, out there, in America and beyond. The task increasingly becomes to remain open to the voices that appear in the contradictions of trying to lead a decent life while being a white American male, and even if poor by current American standards, living with the conveniences that only 1 percent of the world population enjoys.

—February 18, 1978,
Los Angeles.

What She Means

To tense, then bound—

to tense bind time—

its tock

sick ax scent,

Narcissus

loosed
within the urn

grip
of the iron

grp of
the pond strangling i—

centering spider

aligns the voice coil in the magnetic

gap

STUDY FOR A PORTRAIT OF NORMAN GLASS

I could
      have stayed with you,   not simply led
and left you there, that would have seemed ridiculous, since
you went there, asked me to show you the nearest pissoir,
to pick someone up. I keep coming back
to saying goodnight to you, as if I had walked you home,
shaking hands under the street lamp, starting back
down rue Ravignan, glancing back
you alone standing beside the pissoir;
at that moment its shape dilated
confessional, bat winged thing
drizzle of water irrigating its inner iron
crocodile place, temple because you
were to touch another inside, another's
insides, place your finger in
his rent side and believe? For weeks he had been working
toward you, his skin white as those
aligators I recalled above, the flushed ones of that
story, who grew up in New York City sewers, a story
about as probable as what you waited for
a man to come up in your heart
out of your cess a being will emerge
who can love
Norman and who Norman can love
a two-headed man, about as probable as "The Universal Man"

the belief that there was an all-encompassing Being
prior to creation, who Blake
gives the identity of He,

14

though it is supposedly the embodiment of everything.
As soon as "he" falls, asleep,
what is supposedly the female part of him escapes;
if it were truly part of him to begin with why would it have to escape?
That it does means it was
held a prisoner by this supposedly
all-conscious male being
which is the problem of the male ego in regard to the female.

The Fall consists in thinking that the "One" is a He/ness.

To believe that and to live it is to see woman
as oneself, thus insubstantial, not
other who stands between
                              us, but specific
Caryl I returned to that night;

as I tickled her back we floated
out of the apartment and hovered over you.
This is friendship through her,
                              who reflects
us away

from the father need to survive the son;
through her our heads go to mental
war, to change our own lives and not
work our contentions out in the flesh of others.

I see you by your temple. It is clear to me now
the pissoir is only a covering for a misery
that winds and doubles back so deep in man to
a tomb, as at Palenque one climbs the Temple of Inscriptions
then descends within it to the King
buried within, actually bion,
all bion! That a man I believe myself to be
buried within me was my progenitor!
I take this belief out, a crowbar,

what appeared to be a rib, that man built
woman of himself! and toss it clanking against the street.

STUDY OF A SHADOW

He leaves it
and returns to it
like a car
      enters
the garage at night,
waiting for a person to
drive it out.
      I get
into him (or *onto* him—that is how
he experiences it),

    tenuous connection

   I am a driver
   in an empty car
   where there should be
   a driver.

    His shadow
at such discrepancy with his person
that the other
to be with him at all, so frustrated
watching the slippage,
must act—
that is where I err, I step
between him and his shadow,
but it's my moment, not his,
yet if I don't
it's awful to watch a man with his shadow
bagging out, a residue,

17

yet living, as if there were a butchered
still alive creature, completely made of organs,
in that bag which comes out of him where
were he pure animal, a tail might be;
for the shadow
when it is not worn as aura
and thus the contact point between others, is
a bag, the organs it contains
are the person's generative parts,
and I don't mean his kidneys, his liver or even
his guts,
but his mother and father butchered
in the act of creating him.

ETERNITY

I suddenly recall
two months ago thinking
if you die before I do
if I actually gave up my life
could I enter death
and bring you back,
and live with you again?
I saw you fallen and stooped
by you, said
Caryl, I desire to live only with you so much
I have entered death
to encourage you to live on with me.
And my vision tells me you
would be moved, and I would help
you up

we would go along a path for a while,
there would be no money nor mercy
nor even time, we would have to keep going, get
food, eat, make love, sleep, when we could

There is, in this life, something of
this form, I feel it in our plans,
in going to bed at a certain time, schedule,
and it is not the absence of these things,
it is something we will grasp
in this life, hold, in each, know
but know faintly, totally yet faintly

how is that so? totally

yet faintly? It is the hero, entwined
with the heroine, humble, believing in listening
to themselves, a giant form
minute, shadows of windmill staves turning
across grass

32 VARIATIONS ON SHIKI'S "furukabe no sumi ni ugokazu harami gumo"

Cornered in the deserted bell shrine   a rat-colored spider   October   pregnant

Cornered in the deserted bell shrine   October pregnant rat-colored spider

October cornered in the deserted bell shrine rat-colored spider

October cornered in the rat-colored spider pregnant bell shrine deserted

Rat-colored spider   cornered in the bell shrine   deserted October pregnant

Humming loom of the garden   July   magnolia-colored spider

Strung in the old wall   motionless pregnant spider

Waiting in the corner of the German language pregnant spinner

Deserted bell-less shrine in the October pregnant spider

Cocked in the thicket   mustard-colored spider

Cocked in the pregnant spider   rat-color

Dust in the niche   pregnant spider   ancient wall

Through the deserted bell shrine the pregnant spider's cable

Stranger enemy   the spider's   scattering   offspring

Symbol of nothing   spiderless shrine   pregnant bell

Come back   to the wall's   ripped web

Deep throated jaws of the nearly   invisible pregnant spider

Inwardly cocked   blooming spider

Moved by Paul Blackburn the spider-cocoon filled thicket

In the cocoon's vortex mustard-loaded spider

Drab stone wall   crackless pregnant spider

By Hans Bellmer's bedside   Mary Jane shoed spider

Between the near dead and the nearly dead a torn orb

Paul's eyes Bellmer's eyes   a bucket face   spider face

To build for missing Blackburn a spider shrine

The pregnant spider enshrines missing Paul

Don't burn the black ringed spider!

Opaque web   must it speak of Paul?

In the black ringed spider   mustard speck of Paul

Old wall cornered pregnant motionless spider

Pregnant wall motionless old cornered spider

The old wall cornered in the motionless pregnant spider.

PORTRAIT OF DIANE WAKOSKI

I raised myself to
the sill
curious, going through Jack Frost to
Lorca behind him, so hard
to see through this Spanish spirit under
webby ice smiling at me,
then as now, his green eyes and
the bullet hole between them,
man as a murdered brilliant queer
with a soul greater than my father's,
who would adore me through frost;
the strength of the image debilitating
to that lonely little girl
picking her toes off and playing
with the bloody parts in rain so
torrential it
blurs my obsessions, husbands
like filling stations,
mirages, that don't
pump, a long woman
sphinx body crawls
across the desert, as if my
length were water,
hunched
at the Penelope web
I sew and cut, Atropos to
myself, waiting for Clark Kent to unzip,
inflexible
the bed is a wheel on which I turn
debating whether or not to give off a better odor

as the flames I roast in
grow hotter;
I open up like a cave,
all that was my father
runs around like a mouse
on my lips;
lacking the ability to penetrate
the cunt gets filled with paranoia,
I took mine out along this sill
carrying it like a wallet,
the Lorcas streamed out past me,
they headed down to the docks
where my father's ship was just leaving . . .
I keep trying to pull
men out of the stars
where they seem rooted,
I always end up
with a pulled up plant in my hands . . .
So man who I do
meet why do you separate into
astrological abstraction above,
a creature in nightmare below
whose chest I am crouched upon,
my stethoscope
a jar containing
a wasp
cannot sting you into loving me.

POEM COPIED FROM TEXT WRITTEN IN A DREAM

I, Charles Olson,
    left

    Oprecht
    walking my bicycle

    a trace of chat
    on the catless road

     seemed to bridge
    two far points
     moon nodes

    where I'd gotten air
the boy said be sure to see
the north ear
    the marsh there   nothing intersecting earth
                               more beautiful

I cast
& netted
Babson Whitehead
Jung & Neumann
stocked
my inner lake
until I need no longer
want what other men call
food, the outside,
was sufficient on
my innerness
an image of man
& collaged their
words into the fabric
—were they keloid
over an unhealable wound?
A faceless woman
chained to
the Venus of Willendorf
—was the lacuna in
the arete this crouched facelesson

the bridge across

atlementheneira

THE SANDSTONE GATE

for Hayden Carruth

This happened long ago.
He had begun to see himself
instead of what his father saw
or so he thought.
He itched and stank, misunderstanding
the nature of what he was
he brought Maureen his rattles
and his books, thinking if I can just
get in all my troubles will be over.
Maureen said, "you may see me before and
after I see the one I entertain with my
Irish breasts" as she would smile
at what he was, they would read together
by her sandstone gate,
he thought: if I could just stretch myself into a size
to fit that gate
there'd be a warm bath inside
where I might rest
and draw signs of her
on the tub walls forever;
wrenching his mouth apart
got from his chest some cry:
a green cloud prickly and strong with
his stink, this he carried like a crown to her place
and while she was dallying with her suitor
he squeezed it into her milkbox—
yuk, what a poem, she tried to get it off her hands
how vile, and said nothing
for she kind of liked that
half of him looked like an old man

and half mirrored her, she liked
to fantasize two people
making love to her, she dreamed of
herself as another her,
her her's sex grasped her head
while her sex grasped her father's head,
for hours she would lie in the tub
stoned on what seemed the ultimate equilibrium;
meanwhile the one who thought
he had begun to see himself
was like a mouse in her wall,
a tendril she knew sooner or later would poke through.
She considered: he is ceasing to be a dope,
only so much longer can I read with him on the floor
then introduce him for the nth time to my suitor,
or call him late at night when my suitor has left
and invite him to sit with me on the floor until dawn
soulfully missing each instant the point of life—
she knew he wanted in
and that if she let him in he might
not withdraw but go on into her tub
install himself there for good;
well, she found a way, she parted
the silk curtains which appeared to
hang before a window but which actually
covered her great sandstone gate;
with all her might she pressed and pressed
contracting the gate to diaphragm size
and slipped it into her sex where it miraculously
grew phalanges and anchored itself convex
to the outside; he was knocking and she let him in
letting him this time after 10 minutes unhook
her brassiere, a flimsy thing it glowed hieroglyphic
a doily of radium to his eyes crossed in inner itch,
she felt herself picked up and carried to
within inches of what he thought the gate,
she heard him hit, bluebird against her window

then a distant pounding, some neighbor working
on his fender with a rubber hammer

        Crazed he stumbled
out into what was no longer Bloomington
but the ruins of an ancient Hindu city,
he was looking for some salve, something to ease
that ache, the absurdity of looking for ointment in
a rubbled field, but he was still caught up
perhaps more now than ever in his father's
values, everything was dust, he was
fixed about an idea, bent over it, his legs
wrapped around an enormous sandstone gate or goddess
which jerked and bumped around the ruins,
o mother he thought after a while if only
you'd get me off this! presto, there she was, or
as much of her as he might reasonably expect,
a young woman wearing a mask of her
looked up at him and beckoned him into her pit.
He stiffened, the goddess relaxed,
he fell then into a sleep of sensory
deprivation, shapes but no particulars,
he was in the tub but the goddess
had dressed him in rubber so while he floated
he could not feel, or had he ever really felt?
That became his strait-jacket
and he dreamed of Midas, to touch something
into gold since everything *appeared*
to touch him but didn't; there were now two
outsides, that far filmy place called nature
and a closer outside, a one-inch void about him
which far nature seemed filtered through,
author sounds, or radio static,
he dreamed himself to the point Maureen in milk
colored floorlength silk was advancing toward him,
benevolent, her arms outstretched,
he weighed tons crosslegged on the floor

in her corner, since she never reached him,
since he could not rise, his genital city
grew enormous; from his ruling tower
he decreed there were to be two castes of women,
the Emanation and
the Will—the first stayed so close to man, was so
warm and wavy, this caste was allowed to serve,
was treated with compassion and when elderly
was retired to The Palace of The Doves;
the other had severed herself, no longer could
he feel her as something waving out of him,
independent she had power to potentially
oppose him—*oppose* him! He contemplated
The Palace of Entrails in which this caste
would be Iron Maidened.

THE WOMAN WHO SAW THROUGH
PARADISE

---

was squatting in her garden
weeding, many years ago
and also long before her age,
she was two women, one
about 20 in jeans, the other
naked with her body close
to what she weeded, these two in
one discovered a head that day
severed and shrunken, that is
she felt it under a root, thought it
a rock at first
but in pulling it up
she knew it was a head

Then this two in one raced
a long splendid shadow
across the midwest, a goddess
she appeared to men, her clothing
tatters, her feet barely touching
the furrows, she raced because
she cried, frightened and smaller
than the men who felt her like the wind,
and in her crying she crouched
surrounded by a wall of huge men,
that is why she raced,
because she crouched
frightened in her garden
by this head she could hold in
her palm

Now the girl in jeans
took them off and in a kind of
secret ecstasy fit
the face against her cunt,
just to play with it there,
to slime herself,
bored, without a man,
she lay back and rubbed and rubbed
until the head came apart,
feeling funny she dressed
and went back into the stone house;
but this naked other
who was close to
what she worked
looked at the head in disgust,
A poisonous head, she whispered
to herself, it's only time
and the stories I've let get in me,
told by men, that would seduce
me into coming from contact with
this head—if I rub it against me
it will try to take root—
but if it were a woman's head
I would care for it,
cradle it in a sling
which I'd hang from a high beech limb;
if it were clearly a woman's I'd
nurse it and bring it
to a body again, but this
is a mythic head,
its meaning is
the distortion in life,
and she scratched its surface
off, but was stopped
by the skull
which appeared to be male,

she felt another sense of origin was
inside, but her fingers
could not reach it
through the mouth or sockets
so she smashed the head against the beech
that, had it clearly been a woman's head,
she would have slung it from

Then she too returned to the stone house
and found her sister
with many arms, hairy, the jeans
split lying on the floor,
entangled in a skein of stuff
that seemed to issue
from her stomach, sticky, a web
she was either weaving into a
structure, or was she
sewing herself into an opaque
cocoon?

The naked other
sat down below her sister,
she put an end
into her mouth and while
her spider sister sewed
began to eat, it
tasted green
but something else
was in its fiber,
a kind of rotted metal taste
as if the crushed skull were
in her sister's thread,
she saw herself back in the garden
holding the head once more,
as she looked up she felt
the presence of the huge
male will around her

"you are in paradise" it whispered,
now had she been her sister in jeans
she would have heard
"paradise" and felt so glad
for the protected balance between
wildness and domestication
a walled garden meant
—but she was not her sister
nor was she now totally dependent
upon this garden for survival,
she bit off another segment
and heard "paradise"
as "pared eyes" suddenly
nature seemed to be
intent upon her, each
living thing composed of eyes paired
against her, yet the beech boles
were not eyes and although nature
was charged with will
she saw no wall—she felt
outside something that as her
sister self she had before
felt inside, but when
was before? *Before I smashed
the head* she said out loud to
steady herself and went to
the beech to inspect
the place of impact—the trunk
was sheathed in aura,
a grey organ light,
an interaction of the power
the beech sent forth and something
that had been injected into
its aura or
into her mind?
As she tried to discern
this something she felt

35

sick and looked up at her spider
sister in the darkened corner
—the weaving had stopped,
the spider was haggard and
motioned at its mouth, but
what could this naked other
feed it? It was hooked
on the web—she reached down
below her butt and handed up
the only tangible thing she
had to give—this the spider
swallowed and resumed its weaving
—this block seemed to mean:
think it through again,
keep the circuit closed and
moving or the male wall you
have partially opened will
seal fast–she took
the beech aura in her hands
and saw that the injected shadow
was greyish
semen which
interacted with the beech power
opaquing its aura;
out of their impotence before death
men had conceived this specific
image making force to establish
origin as male and offer
women themselves as consequence and
as generation, responsible yet
secondary; such appeared to be the content
of the will she felt surrounding
her, a world made by men
for themselves and for women which,
when she crouched in the garden,
was calculated to evoke paradise,
which when closely examined

was a skin that
kept her and her sister self
at one remove from what raced
through nature, a woman
never really glimpsed
but there, a thrill through the air,
a part of what is green,
a fluid in the night and
the day, a contour to the blackness
and the light
which now streamed into
the stone house illuminating
the spider sister, its web
littered with corpses, a chalice
of blood in one claw, a scimitar
in another as it danced
in place, a dead stiff cock
inside it, the engine of
its dance! With one hand
the naked other picked up
the edge of this destroyer image
and peeled it like a bandage
from her creative self—
she took the head this self
now offered her, it was a
shining wet thing, beyond
generation—she grasped it
firmly then snapped it open,
her brain! She looked at
the coiled snake from which
the male caul had been
removed, stunned she carried
it outside to the beech sling.

THE MALE WILL

had to claim beginning,
why not here it
thought, where her pod
leashed
my fountain to my misery.
Say she was pulling
drops
from my vertical leverage,
I rise and
I rise, always
a falling
short, a
sky I can only get so
far into, reverse
this gravity
against a center,
stick
gender
onto
night,
layer the day,
restratify
the ground
I rot in, midden
hear it maiden,
inject neuter
with razors of
he/she,
there must be
a reason why I

happen to me,
since none of the yolk
strung out in the thicket
can be egg
ever again
I will create a place
even the zero
comes from, instead
of my being curled
inside her with the earth
outside, I will encompass
her and the earth,
woman as merely
the oar between
grip and ocean,
a tool
by which
I stroke
myself along.

VARIATIONS DONE FOR GARY SNYDER

At the point the earth contracts, a beautiful emphasis?
Consciousness, a two-way street by a one-way polluted stream,
iced stream flowing into a birth, I started to say a bridge,
    I started to say Driving along that dream north of Kyoto
    Station,
Barbara was there, we didn't know where we were going,
the grasp for one phrase to make you see
    what I will never see again, new country
tangled in the legs I am crossing and uncrossing in my lap

At the point consciousness reverses, a tree turns within its own bark?
Have I spat out Clayton while the polluted sky mainlined the beech?
Have you, Gary, integrated Kitkitdizze while the eel
    can no longer regurgitate Mercury?
At the point the earth contracts, do we suddenly see how we can live?

The spiderweb dangles vulva-outward its fibers,
    an 80 year old man sleeps on the sidewalk,
becomes conscious as a sun-tentacle gropes his eyes,
for that man the ray was "the most beautiful sunrise I have ever seen"
    Not an aggression, but a filmy dragon of reception,
The storks at play in the lotus pond,
The immense need of the Chinese to feel the peach
    swollen with jade, to feel that each
movement must be justified, aligned, by its contrary,
that the Red Lotus Peak must be imbued with juice
    from under a woman's tongue,
the Double Lotus Peak must carry the meaning of milk
    spit from tits unchildsucked,
the Peak of the Purple Fungus ah! hides the Grotto of the White

Tiger,
gateway upon gateway, and all blemished, all foregrounded,
    by a woman's bound and festering foot . . .

I try to hold in mind one thought: the earth in contraction,
an LA backyard of pastel screens in which the fir and lemon tree,
    parts of a set,
can be moved into a film or be replaced by a person,
Rebirth so passionately meaningful,
    in the orgone accumulator
overgrown with ivy, the goat-god couples with darkness,
the brothel walls of Pompei so faded one can hardly hear
    his hoarse chortle,
Not a contraction like a blow in the stomach or even a birth wince,
the ache a feeling of the grass growing in each blade more narrow,
so the poetic line narrows, there is less concentration on
any one focus, movement is freer, horror is skipped over,
we don't have to contract, as Baudelaire did, plum blossom poison
or be possessed by maggots with Greek statues in their arms,
    Ixcuina the Aztec inspiration crouched,
    a world then utterly open it seems now
but they would cut a woman's lips off her face
about as fast as I threw a squeezed lemon half at Caryl.

    So does it contract or stay, in world movement, static?

    Scales flake from fish now,
    given the form Mercury has assumed,
    "the pansie freakt with jet"   no longer Milton's flower
luminescent with black, yet no way to know
if we come from a greater time or go toward one—
    but the contraction, the death of the infinite,
plants seeds of a new infinite in the increasingly mortal
    torch all things now carry,
    your dove flies not only straight toward the mast
but in the upheaval in the air, perches,
    its own dovecot, sterile yet

saddled with ticks, as if anything could define
    what we feel embracing
    finding we are all eyes in the chalk stem.

IXCUINA

I find myself running through
the streets of Tenochtitlan, a messenger
I pass many people in stocks,
I come from something in my hand, everything
is brown, tan, the stocks the people,
there is blood in the streets
but it isn't bad, I am where
the rational pavement gives
way to a fluid, I am swimming in the street
with my message, I know Tenochtitlan,
does this lead me to Ixcuina? Because I am in
a dream I fear I cannot control
my turns, any second I could be back
in Indianapolis eating Sunday dinner at
"The Hawthorne Room" any second the dirt
street I am swimming through could dump
me before the hostess while my father
slowly parks our car . . .

But that is no longer a problem
because I am no longer a model for Ixcuina,
I circulate in its chambers, water
dashed through the interior of a statue,
in a flash I have flowed through
while I am still running through Tenochtitlan,
the charge is to not stop dreaming
while I am awake, to be conscious in my dream
while I relax enough so the street
is fluid, I am sure I delivered the message
long ago and am free in a sense to

explore Tenochtitlan, but if I stop to ask why
of someone in the stocks I risk waking,
the point is to be here and there, and here
has two places too, to be in the poem and
wherever between the dream and poem is.
My dream is of a prior civilization that goes on
over the Ibuki's benjo, a man in a birth crouch
who wanted to write but who
without his dream, having not recreated his dream,
had to shit; Ixcuina has a smaller
version of itself tunneling out between its thighs,
the telegram I am carrying has the form
coming out never getting free,
I stand on that, it is not to merely be with the form
but neither to behold the form outside
its conjunction with me, Ixcuina
toward which all of me presses
makes me partially visible, I adhere to
Ixcuina, that is, I live most fully
in the poem and the point is not to be wrapped
around it like someone hiding the globe
nor to view it, a critic, as something
departed, imagine being in parturition
all the time! Ixcuina is not female, it is an image
not a man or a woman posing
in birth or in mockery of birth,
I flow now without impediment towards it.

SATURDAY EVENING

The carrot puree stuck to the moulinette,
vital orange on inert stainless steel,

yet I have read all things flow
and maybe that is part of the reason
people pollute because they see as Heraclitus
and Michael McClure nature as a fire.
Some things do not burn.

I eat too much and enjoy the meal
served with good wine.
So pleasure is always more than one needs?
If you were really in touch a voice of Snyder tells me
you would leave the city system and be more
than a dome wart on a hillside.
My maroon carpet-bag jacket
hangs on the closet door knob a pleasure
somewhat like the carrot puree,
neither essential
are part of the structure I live in.

More and more people hunt
people who sustain people,
thus psyche is complicated, estranged,
while the shark is increasingly slick,
an actor in a film, clots of oil
plastered to its teeth.
Since man will have his pabulum
he needs something cuddly to squeeze,

Donald Duck, understandable, no?
People eating the lowest class of people,
that cannibalism possible
in the structure of this Saturday evening,
an ad portraying Vincent in his grey felt hat
on the rear door of a van
and the opened skulls bolted into the lie of a center
where Cronus, having finished eating,
watches the new Ford van go.

A CLIMACTERIC

for Maroin Kassab Bachi

Today I surprised my parents in profile,
I watched them flinch
as if they had been shot and then carefully wrapped
like a hot revolver, a warm autumn dawn,
Indianapolis 1934.

Today I walked into my tomb,
into my breakfast, her surrounding nourishment.
I watched the neck of the plant,
the cogollo between root and bud,
the sulphur in the test tube
as he soured in her and she sweetened
shuddering behind her confession.

Today I realized I will no longer
dream of her turning aside
and beckoning me to their bedside.

I have just realized it would be natural
for her to want me to be close to her
as what I am begins to seethe in her being,
in her background, in her bassinet with
its winding sheet blowing abandoned in the woods.

I have just realized her abject
loneliness as his weight shifted,
poised, and then took off like a loon
through only part of her sky,
have just accepted her invitation to
unbutton by her head so she could see

the part of him I came through while
I was coming through

yoked
to her sound I never before remembered.

IRA

a leaf, a weightlessness, a brother who never was,
　　a little companion who never was,
fence post before Clayton, companion only of Jr.,
invisible for 40 years now simply a lost leaf, one
　　of thousands in the driveway,
a Piglet, a natal demon standing with snow cap pulled
　　down so I cannot see his face,
I cannot tell if he is smiling under, or if his face is chewed
　　up into an expression of fury,
fist-face, battered vegetable face, with a stone behind it
　　or a present? Where did you come from?
Who sent you to my house? Surely you must be like me
　　for I cannot play with anyone different than me,
surely you must have been sent by my mother, and if so,
must be my brother, for my mother would not send someone
　　she herself did not have . . .
I must go out to you since it is so silent in my room and
　　so beautifully silent in the deep snow
where you stand, little herm, boundary marker between her
　　and me, chum, little faceless one,
do you love me? She must have known I was lonely, surely
　　that is why she sent you, or
planted you in the snow, she must have felt me become a singular
　　foetus in her, of all the goldenrod my father sowed
she must have felt you and thousands like you drown in the dust
　　of her organs and leave her, an only mother with child . . .
So long have I tried to blind you out of my consternation
　　not knowing what you
were going to do to me, surely you must have seen me emerging
with my face from which a blowtorch was flaming, was that

why you pummeled me in the snow? But we could not
      have emerged hand in hand,
I was to be single, with you tacked to my chest,
planted so close you are involved with my most intimate laughter.

THE DRAGON RAT TAIL

for Norm Weinstein

Where my hope, naive
and controled by a roteness
thought art might be
a single Japanese flower
deft in a bowl, my hope
to escape profusion,
a single flower, a red gleam,
one thing alone against
clay and wood—
    a poem began to grow
in the very room with
that wilting flower,
but it was an atmosphere of
a poem can be,
a poem is around here,
I took hold
between my crosslegged
legs of a string of rain,
it was to find something to pull
out, to put
into my mouth
an ancient story,
to find where
my tale began and pull
up, too physical
I knew, so physical
I would have to digest
the having of
a cock, gnaw
the archetype through,

51

the body
was good
but was attached
to an image I
could only sense, a rat
growing in the tatami,
I pulled
on a growing widening tail,
a construction worker
pulling an endless aligator out of a sewer,
but through the tatami itself,
hideously embarrassed by
the closeness of the thing,
whatever it was, to my
own organs, that I was pulling
myself inside out, that the poem
I sought was my own menstrual
lining, as if suddenly one day
I would have my inside
out on the tatami before me,
a kind of flayedness, a cape,
something in words, but words
hooked together an anguish or
covering, a quilt, as if
Indianapolis had been pulled off
and the rawness remained,
flickering off and on off my nerves,
jagged aura, some of it grey
some of it blue, and under?
The rigidity pit
where Clayton and Gladys sweetly
wandered, looking up
in intense innocent
complicity with an image
I moved into, then out, then into in
their eyes, that is when Kelly cried
"Find them in the grass!"

he meant find the mothering
fathering powers which are not
your mother, father, find
and connect to what they are
the ghosts of—
I glimpse the doppelgänger
they as well as I
were involved with,
personal and cultural
shadow in diamond light
striding across a stage.
The scales increased—
a long green thing was
piano practice, apprenticework
took 16 years, diurnal,
inside the day the impossible
spine of saying all
that the day was
blocked me, I bent,
spine, over keys,
inside the machine a Christmas tree
glowed, and under it
puberty subincision,
I posed, by my dog, he
went off into the night,
I tried to reach a Japanese bar hostess
through my morality play,
my father pressed the flash-bulb,
Rilke fell out, compassionate,
distant, paper . . .
Rote screw-hive
alive but compressed into "God"
Days of sitting on the bench
and trying to bank a word
free from the roar of never
that quietly gnawed, given
my hold to the tail

which had not grown,
which had grown enormous—
"the moment of desire" Blake calls
it, break the judge
in highchair, bring that Jack Horner
that "Good boy" satisfied with
his plum dipped thumb into
the savage truth of this world:
people want love
only as a passive given,
they hate and actively
oppose love as an active opposition.
In Kyoto, faced with my dragon
rat tail I understood that the world
was adamant, that there is no way through it.
Gates, philosophies, arts, all "ways"
confronted orange mud running down
a twilit road on Sunday afternoon.
One way to get anything out: haul up
and sieve, engage the haul,
make the rat tail big, dragon tail,
make the dragon tail bigger than Jung,
bigger than all ideas,
let it engorge the house,
split the tatami! Ride
it! Not the moon, not
the nostalgia for that other place,
but the funk that struck inside
on the way home from the public bath.
Not to remember or realize the bath.
Be in the bath. Deal
with this other thing, art does not have to
lip the natural, live the natural,
jack off on her fender if I have to but
live the natural and confront
this other thing, sieve out
the little performer,

break the piano bench I was to become
an alcoholic upon, "Blue Moon"
"White Christmas" a chain of command,
break the chain, open it up and discover
the seed-chum she and he and all of them,
the whole atavistic octopus,
pumped into my wine cup, be
paranoiac, splay out, feel spiderlike
throughout the realm that paranoia
seeks to feel, understand the rigidity
pit is armor, something
I can get rid of,
yet it is bone, what
I stand in,
armorless armor,
my marrow, my
very scent, is
social, where I do not have to be,
where I am forever, as long as I
am alive, packed in with
who I am born with, alone or
brothered, essentially with the ghosts of
the fathering mothering powers I
can transform to aid me.
My mother's dead eyes float out
bald in raving love for me,
how she knew what she wanted me to be
so confused was she in what I should be,
under every fried egg, every Boy Scout knot,
under the Betty Grable butt allowed on my closet door,
under the ghost games under the bed Saturday afternoon,
under my being allowed
to dress up in her girdle and twirl
the family safe, was Liberace, the person
she hoped I would be, fully middleclass,
artistic, gay, fully in command, a hero
wrapped in a 146

pound floor length black
mink cape lined with Austrian rhinestones,
a ghastly Virgil!

  Confidence
I pray, at 40, to lead this doppelgänger out to pasture,
he cannot be done with,
I can only let him graze,
I am his shepherd, linked to
him Americanwise through Harlem,
through Chile, through Iran.

DAILY

A paper-clip
a lamp and
a bottle of "Liquid Paper"
on my desk—
                    the clip edges glint
in the lamp light at 4 PM
"Liquid Paper" so
contained in its little jar—
I look up
dust on the lamp's stone breasts,
                    my face close enough
to the bulb to feel its warmth,
                    any area
of the desk there is a place,
a little whirlpool
in which Caryl stands,
even though she is gone
during the day these days,

I pick up her striped
panties on the bedroom floor,
why don't I write about the intimate things
I really love, I think, dropping them in the hamper,

she smiles from the whirlpool
go ahead.

You are here so thoroughly
the male d in God is softened.

DUMMIES

Charlie Manson seated on Edgar Bergen's knee,
a beat up, badly fed, withered
punk; they're at a party in Bel-Air,
Charlie says: "Wanna know how to
break a young woman's will, Bergen?
Make her suck some guy's dick all
day long, all day long, from sunrise to
sunset, while I rest against a rock
and try to think myself out
of this dummy, like why
I only say what you
think is funny, that is
I don't have a life
because I am spoken through,
you know, authors in eternity,
Cocteau in the guise of Orpheus
hunched before a car radio copying
stock reports, or Spicer up all night
waiting for the Martian delivery—
'all day long' is the key,
in 12 hours you can kill the ego
and then the archai
all start shoving their way in,
it's like a sale, hundreds of women
trying to get at the dresses and panties,
only it's the young woman's mind they're buying,
like is this piece only $1.59?
So they rummage through her,
get all the pieces that fit,
finish their shopping, bus back home,

start cookin supper, the husband wanders in,
'Hey honey y'oughta see what
I got down at Susan Atkins' today'
And she wears it right out on the street—but
you guys, Bergen,
you've got the luscious cuts,
the originals are on your wives!"

ASSASSIN

Pulled up my birthday
plant and as instructed
stabbed it in its roots,
then hung by its roots its power
would flow into
its head

      I hang
in my closet a hanged
man glowing between my
shirts and pants

smoked I roll
Eshleman's head
around on the earth

What to do with his body
—this is marijuana's song—
what to do with his body
while around on the earth
I roll his head

STILL-LIFE, WITH MANSON

There is a scene in the film called "The Damned"
in which the SS replaces the German Standing Army.
Some of the bored Army youths have dressed up like can-can girls
to entertain their beer drinking companions in a lakeside roadhouse.
Now late at night everyone is in a stupor except
one dancer in black
net hose, smoking,
looking out into the lake darkness . . .
It is always very quiet right before the gun-boats appear
filled with Kali Krishnas whose putt-putt can be
heard as Tex Watson makes the final turn, 10050 Cielo Drive,
12:10 AM. That hard thigh coated with hose
was the screen onto which I
and my Indianapolis friends were projected, ant
ticks in the pompon machine, our destruction
intimate with our growth. We were joined
by the death of whatever surge there was in puberty,
Charlie Manson, an altar,
over which, spread-eagled, his heart was
torn from his chest and held to the sun,
and the sun, extending what I can only describe as a goiter-filled
viper-coiled claw, took his little boy heart, tasted it, grimaced,
and spat the tasted bit back into his face.
For us, survival was assured.
After classes Friday afternoon we'd
get some beer, park in back of the church and tell
dirty jokes to the girls, unaware
that in our titilated numbness Charlie was casing
house after house for the punch line
onto which his spat back joke fit.

61

STILL-LIFE, WITH FRATERNITY

for Ted Grieder

In dream, enormous tree-house, led up to by a ladder, a hive of sorts,
the distance to the ground below frightening.
In the top of the hive, bunk to bunk the pledges and actives, like cakes
in an oven, all the same, or so we seem to me still, in the dreams going
   on
then, a "still-life" but even if stilled, still life. Below,
as if hundreds of feet below, there were actives awake working
out an earlier dream—the pledges were to be aroused from sleep,
driven down the ladder and beaten at the base of the tree,
the tree-house fraternity contracting and expanding,
at one moment it is the frail one I built 15 feet over the sidewalk next
    to 4705
and then it is a relative mansion, my "Grand Central Station" where
I talk with my mother and try to keep out
of the dream a certain maniacal presence,
we are always at the bottom of a staircase
with simonized relatives slipping around us,
all oak, very wooden, warm at that base, a neurotic
launching-pad, deep in-firing cyst poised in the limbs or floating
high in the air, from which a root of smoke dangles

                        I must descend
when they shout for me, as if I were ripped
from my Siamese twin

Below Dunn's farm where the fratfire plays,
Jay Christy is screwing Bunny MacCrory,
several months later his car is out there alone,
I pull up, he wiggles out beer in hand, "Laura" is on the radio,
his girl-friend is sitting in the front seat in a wash-basin

he found in the Phi Delt kitchen, her bottom
wet in abortioned ooze. Christy and I carry the basin behind his car,
look at it in my headlights, we can't tell if its all come out yet.
We might as well have been looking into a mirror
or have been two stone lawn cherubs holding up a bird bath—the
        focus
belonged to the brotherhood, we were searching for pieces of flesh.
All rites of passage, whether well or poorly conducted,
bend the individual soul into the will of the nation or tribe,
and mine is the ghost back of Phi Delta Theta
screwing Bunny back into the woodwork out of which at
17 years old she timidly put forth her sex,
Christy fixes his screwdriver into her slot
he turns her back into matter
tosses the screwdriver into the trunk and walks away

What is virgin or just beginning to be experienced
is destroyed before it is fully there.
In ceremonies that pretended to carry us across
from being boys to being men the actual transition
was from a pledge trembling in bunny-footed p.j.s at a midnight
        "line-up"
to an active with a paddle pinned to a girl from a good sorority,
TV holding hands Saturday evening or when the weather was good
the fratfire at Dunn's farm with songs,
that maniacal presence where the pines began
as if our relative, Manson, wanted to join us, all bloody wanting
to be part of our evening

Bunny MacCrory, split under the force of the bore
regardless of how tentative it was,
now had an upper and a lower life,
now the tiny Phi Delt sword could be tucked
through her cashmere sweater nipping her bra
while her discarded lower parts cooked for us, the mammy in our
        basement,
or crouched behind the house in the bushes Sunday evening

willing to blow whoever found out she was there

What remains can be seen Sunday after church and Sunday dinner,
the pledges are kind of grubby, they have no time to do their own
    laundry,
the actives are imperial, they pose against the limestone or
toss footballs while the girls who are under them
wait. There is no time in this moment, the leaves'
shadow stops—the suits we are wearing, the utter
outerness of our lives translates itself out into our most inner
problems; we are not just kids wandering around in sport coats and
    ties,
we are our own aura, you can see in us at our edges supple
brown snake skin shoes, Christy favors a sable brown brass buttoned
    blazer,
without any difficulty of transition we are models posed on phantom
    jets
for Harper's Bazaar 1965 "What America Does Best"
khaki wool tweed opening on a burst of orange.

STUDY FOR A PORTRAIT OF HANS BELLMER

A cephalopod
center that puts out spike-heeled tentacles floats by
coiling and smiling,
where her buttocks converge is the puberty
tube of the 12 year old
just beginning to hair tiny tentacles,
and in the tube, a spider
poised under its trap-door,
Death holds her sex in its teeth
and all of her shrieks out expanding her octopus ghost,
it floats off and leaves another young girl
sitting in my sandbox
legs spread, playing with her archangelic toy,
she puts ants on it
as if to recapture an old old dildo,
her paleolithic cream-stick,
before God broke it off to fuck her
and the octop-eye was born.
She pokes pencil holes in her toy
and fashions inside it curling stairways,
vast brick hallways which diminish to boot-shaped exits—
no one there but her fingers and the baffled ants,
they feel their octopus sister as Bellmer's
concentration probes
the erector-set tower in that toy,
all the childhood marvels are crossed
by these ants, their antennae done up in hair-bows,
their earth odor overcome by powdered menthol,
they wander and become the dildo bone,

an archangelic pulse trembles the trees,
Bellmer has hidden below a path on which
Nazis are tramping, hush!
they come by, the professors,
the soldiers, they carry the 12 year old like dug up train ties,
like the house of life, they march under her lumber,
the woman is being carried, beam by beam back
into an invisible Black Forest.

*

In another part of that woods,
Bellmer approaches a mill
where light hardly ever reaches—
a woman is sitting
by the wheel, her lizards rush into the shadows,
she is about 20 to judge by one foot,
about 10 to judge by the other
"You want the youth of woman,
Bellmer, to the exclusion of her maturity,
you want me to dance on your disembodied cock
like a bear on a ball, proud that you have the mercy not
to drag me off onto a surgical table.
I hate you and your needle-fingered marionettes, your dragonfly
fft fft everytime you smell me move,
behind your octopus image of me is not merely a parrot beak
but everything else in the world you have asphyxiated
to concentrate on your dilated obsession."

Bellmer stood, and holding his eyes
between his lips blew the whites into her pond.
His pupils remained at the edge of a void;
between initiation and end-effect,
there is a table that does not always
want to be loaded with buttocks—it would like to have
a jug with some flowers, a worm
to follow, rose petals over Bellmer and Unica Zurn.

The table, the lumber, want to unman and be
allowed, to not always be shadowed by people's assholes.

Bricks
Selfphallicpods

van Gogh's armchair with a candle
    update: a stool
            out of which a
            cock fastens
                the lady sitter spread

doll body empty ball shells
mortared hairbow

mannequin junky

from so much mindless fucking:
fashion talk   flaring
                    tongue to
                stacked heel

THE COGOLLO

for Theodore Enslin

Driving back from your reading at Irvine,
knowing Reich's orgastic potency has become self-regulation for me
and I am stuck with it, a truth like a match a crow throws and lights
against the rock, they laugh "have a better orgasm!" ha ha
written as my mother used to, she did not know how to tell some-
    thing funny,
ha ha the laughter of the billions who support love-yearn anxiety,
"gratified" they say, good orgasms yah, a moment later they are
    again
those billions gulping the sex bait, they say "orgasm"
as if that dim sublime makes up for the failure of two people
to create the sacred, moisten the atmosphere around them,
where the contradictions, the revilements, the self-doubts and self-
    pity
are burned, so that the elves and archai,
linked paperclips of energy, are revitalized in the air around us.
Having taken off our corsets and 19th century
headgear, how perplexing it is, to feel media
slipping the power out of language as one might debone
a chicken before the remaining flesh is roasted, eaten, done with,
and to realize too that Reich is but one aspect of a point
slowly being opened, a black spot in the lives of people 100 years ago
when children's hands were tied to the bedposts at night
and husbands never once saw their wives naked,
when masturbation on the part of young girls was actually punished
    by
excising the girl's clitoris. "You are so beautiful . . ."
the radio crooned this afternoon, driving down Wilshire,
I was seeing the linked paperclips, realizing how they had become
spaceships for Reich, how beautiful that he had put

that much into the air, had given the air almost
what it had given him as he struggled into his 57th year
while the FDA spent 10% of its budget to feed him into prison and
    literally
break his heart. I hear in that crooning "beautiful"
the Nazi current running obliquely through America,
adoration of the flesh as a thing in itself,
Miss America turns on her platter, I see stadiums of Nazi
Youth stoned on calisthenics, their strong well-tended bodies
doing jumping jacks on a black
Indian's back, he is pulling
mussels from a baked field which are his dinner, I so free by
    comparison
walk into my bedroom and look at the unmade double pillowed bed
touched by the soft sculpture of a blanket poised in the bend Caryl
    left it
when she got up this morning to get dressed for work—fidelity
the most beautiful thing on earth, but do I convey it
using that radio word? How closely everything
is packed in spoonwise with its opposite, the grass
is full of Donald Duck, a cartoon of what everyone does to each other
doing ha ha to each other. Orgasm as gargoyle,
a split spewer that juts from cathedral edge,
heretical companion; in the tension of the missing orgasm
men created Paradise and they stand in circle,
a huge wall around that gap focusing their rage
on its most precious human contrary, a pussy
white and frightened leaps around before them like a bunny.
Men live at a never ending sexual funeral
where their ripped away Siamese twin is the stuff in the casket,
when they look closely he is the remains of a paleolithic
bison, their real double, their 50% other, the animal
they lost in their cavity when eons ago they descended
the pyramid's inner stairway to become ha ha immortal.
Knowing remains a procedure
instead of the knower revealing the process through which
his living is connected to what he knows, yet

69

the cogollo, "the heart of the cabbage, the shoot of the plant,
the summit of pine" need not be missing.
At the core of my poetry, where my mother is buried,
I dream the strength of my yearning toward oneness,
when the critics of the day
become the succubi of 4 AM
I think them aside and conserve my strength for the morning,
love, made, keeps me living in the poem and the poem,
to remain pregnant in birth, tumbles me out on the shore
to illuminate, with Caryl again, antiphonal.

CHRYSANTHEMUM LANE

A house at the bottom of a canyon
by a brook, hollyhocks, a
cottage at the bottom of the page
in a child's book, I still
smell the wood ink odor of
that process, that sunbeam
gurgle of blonde curls
a little Caryl with her book of ages
standing before Thou Shall &
Shall Not, cleft rock
in which I still dream flowered
cottage, farawayland
sunbeam & toast, it sets
dawnlike, an agate in my hope.

ALLELUIA CHORUSES

Clifford Brown
Philadelphia, June 25, 1956
Night in Tunisia and *Donna Lee*
triple-tongued as if the
trumpet lived in his lips,
he spit
shyly the melody off
his structure, cleaning it
minorly, keeping the created
non-melody of two tunes alive,
"You make me feel so, uh
wonderful . . . I really must go now, it's so
hot!" then went off into Pennsylvania
Turnpike invisibility,
his trumpet
which he clutches
pressed to his black
slave heritage
as it meshes with repetition
rowing in galley,
prove prove prove,
a substructure, chord skeleton
over which the flesh
scampers or hangs itself in ballad.

With no rhythm section behind
or chord structure under
Rilke's jaundiced flame,
the I I know
tender in a niche,
must say itself,
be conscious of

several corrugated
persimmons under, a shrine
where otherwise there were only cold
rock and repetition,
a carnival silo with black
angels riding motorcycles
horizontally gripped to the inner
walls, over bewildered lions and under the
gawking titilated "humans"
gazing down
prove prove that you are
one, prove the chords at fault,
create a fault in
them, let what you have been given slide into
the crevice the chords
allow, bobbin, increase
your whirl about yourself
until you split that rock that
given center that "she"
must invade. Centuries of rock
in man's will against
her active participation
in the crucial space between
his life and her poem.

The aura the armored woman wears
invades the man, who
maintaining his moat, does not
let her in to his precious Keep
where his organs boil in hysterical need,
Easter,
how I looked forward to
that chance to affirm, he is arisen!
Hallelujah Chorused,
transcendence works
downward in the "spine flute,"
I have not lost the Christ-snakes

in my spine I set out to unpack,
they writhe and flash up and down my 12 year old
spine, oiling my spine,
snacking off my spine
as they drum in praise,
raze the word to see what
remains of the word, I just felt a razor
slicing from my spine the tiny film-images
which in aggregate might
reveal hell as packed into praise
one's way out of hell,
this body container, this temporal
and eternal puberty that wants to
prove genital explosions,
Night in Tunisia, against that
morning in Lima, 1965,
the Cantagayo barriada was being
destroyed, *Donna Lee*,
against the Indian woman who kneads
and rakes over rocks in the
flesh-blue pump overflow
what was crushed between two
scimitar moons on the Pennsylvania Turnpike,
Clifford's labyrinth,
his Krishna body
—it *is* an ax, it did fell
a tree shaped silence, which led me
to look down into the strata
of my white Presbyterian legacy
where Clifford rows along my spine,
the alleluia under
the "mysterium tremendum."

AND NOW?

"I see more & more clearly the human form   [Eluard]
still without features & yet
in a dark corner where the wall is"
"straw on which they lay, putrid   [Reska Weiss]
from their urine and excreta, their frozen limbs
fetid and covered with wounds and bites to
the point of bleeding, women, their eyes
glazed from long starvation, countless lice nested in the pus,
their hair was very short, but armies of lice found a home in it,
only three or four were called out daily to be"
glimpsed by Eluard
"without features"
What happens to those who perished in
actual Hell—Hell no longer a millennial dream—
Does what killed them remain?
Is it in our deathly architecture?
In the crap roadside food the driver bored
senseless by the freeways wobbles off for?
It does
go on, part of an emerging "human form?"
Or is it an inversion now, living cups of lice
dragged into fire, so that the mind today
backs off from imagination (so packed is it
with these tortured-to-death),
builds Monopoly game "houses"
dense with contraction, matter all the way through;
imagination, which in essence is grotesque
(all kingdoms coupled)
must accomodate those "glazed of eye
from long starvation"   seed pods
carried forth by survivors.

SCORPION HOPSCOTCH

Unexpectedly this morning I grasped
my orgasm and held it for a moment in my hands,
outwardly a crystal ball—yet as I looked
I penetrated my own reflection and glimpsed
its marvelous inner workings, death
was happy there, a gold fluid that streamed
through the crystal complexity of what I saw,
happy because without orgasm it was forced
to hammer at my back, as if I were death's door,
around death's fluid were many tiny insects,
flies, spiders, even little grubs who seemed to be
nursing at the teats of what was passing through,
they gave death a furry quality, made it more solid
feeling, as if what I see of nature outside of orgasm
was nourished by invisible death—but it was not as if death
"lurked" in the act as Berdyaev and Bataille have said,
a scorpion to sting the lovers when they open that wide,
but flashed across what seemed a winning line, as if death
won a race then that otherwise had it pounding at my back,
and around the insects a feeling of mooing, a low animal
sound density that pressed against the crystal limits,
inhabiting them in a kind of roller-coaster rhythm,
an animal cushion, sharp, breathless and slow, between
the nursing insects and the sudden
reappearance of our bedroom.

THE SPIDER BRIDE

The critic sits down at a small table to read his paper.
René Char is very important to him for reasons I cannot understand.
The words bound by me, elegant basketballs,
as if there were a cereal called Char and this man
were pouring it into my bowl, instantly disappearing snow.
He pours with great feeling, he wants us to be porous to something
between his words and the words of Char whose French states
"We have crushed the eyes of the lion."
The critic thinking he has translated
the line quotes it in English as "blinded the lion."
Certainly he has "crushed the lion's eyes!"

A collapsed man, frill on a pile of filth, picks up
a concentration camp fishhead and starts to suck out its eyes . . .

the lion is stopped before the critic's back.
Walks away. Back in the UCLA classroom
the lion is stopped before the critic's back.
What may or may not be its eyes are blindfolded.
Its way of standing seems to say: "Why has that
which has survived in me been blindfolded?
He makes me wear this, because
he will not look into my crushed eyes."
The lion springs, rips open the critic's back and bounds inside,
for a moment the critic's whole body is rubber mask
and I glimpse the deadliness of reductive clarity:
he is married to a nursery rhyme
who every morning walks from their cottage to the woods
where seated on her tuffet she starts to eat her egg,
but every morning for 20 years a spider bride,

on crutches, has hobbled over to her side—
she shrieks, runs home and remains inside
all day, flustered and sincerely dusting.
Every evening the critic returns, using an outside
stairway which gives him and his female students
direct access to the Upper Room. "This is my body, this my blood"
he says, "feed off me." They press around the table as if
toward him but centripetally toward the sucked out fishhead's eye.
Each is concerned about her unoiled virgin lamp but more concerned
about her grade. Every evening the critic
spreads out his map of last rhetoric before them.
Sometimes they hear what seems to be the spider bride
moving along on her crutches toward the Upper Room.

BARTER

On the radio this noon
terrorists fail to murder Idi Amin—
and were caught.

My orgasm made useless back on the bed
like a dust storm in place,
a black-hearted cyclone . . .

right now, on the other side of the earth,
several men are being sawed into.

Down the dusty path through the village
within feet of their cries
Donald Duck and his nephews whistle along.

The buried treasure they seek,
fresh corpses, not gold coins
but mold on bones that
in time turns back into

a fig,
for a comic book,
in an African boy's palm.

1945

19th century work table
J. Henri Fabre encircled
until the weight of his curiosity
wore path in the stone floor
I follow,
in deepest sincerity,
my path around
the eyes of the Auschwitz survivor
gold barren water,
not a water of everlasting life,
a water to make people puke up
whatever strains of everlasting life were left in them . . .

It might be a water that said live!
—like gold in the mouth.
I raise it to my face from the sink
more refreshing than air.

I see my spirit and its assassin crossing over a hill,
I hear a third power, that survivor,
assert himself, from inside
the hill—not dead but not alive
in the way my spirit and assassin are alive.

Make this survivor visible
in this hill over the basement of 4705,
let the furnace ray up into his barrow
as if he were the life in our American home,
the joists in the first floor, Albion,
what is contactable of "our father"

not a fake barbed
sensation in the wallpaper
but the white father, white as pine,
white
time, an infiltration from Europe's
refusal to die.

THE GREEN APPLE PHOTO

The love in your eyes Caryl
you look at me
and against that looking—
that yearning—that being—
other art is pictures.
I have a Tantrik diagram,
a reproduction, with me,
which set next to
this photo of you is
a mechanical cartoon.
Yet until now I took it
as seriously as I "took"
your photo. You rain
on in me. What falls
is my own, you've
given everything,
you offered all and against
your photo only I
here can enable the rain
to continue falling.
Why do I want to cry
looking at you looking at a camera
with me in mind?
I want to offer you something
away from you. That I
have no need to offer you
with you—because
you never make me look
for my tears! I take too
much for granted in an

assumption that the Tantrik
postcard means something
that is any addition
to you. Away for a month.
Your utter accessibility,
your head tilted under green apples.
Your sweetness, sweetness,
your tart light
heartsown, your hair blown
sweetness, I pause
in the thought that
you offer yourself to me,
while I am here.

Frenstat, Czechoslovakia, 8 July 1976.

OLD JEWISH CEMETERY

Broken off teeth
of the ground,
the jumble
death is, a wrecked
race, entangled
Paul Celan,
twigs, dust, high walls—
the hurricane
has passed through.
So overgrown
I thought of the little woods
next to 4705
looking at my body
the body of Alice Jones 12
that hot
insect haze of looking
for what in
the body?
Tomb upon tomb,
tilted, badgered,
half-submerged (tram
passing—soft
Sunday roar),
the weight of the bottom of
these slabs, to
hold them up
indecipherable
leaned against trees,
collapsed
fences, a field of

collapsed fences,
little ivied trees
(tram again passing
the stone my butt is on
quivers), I'm at
the most ill kept
end of the cemetery
—German and American
tourist groups at the other.
Without order, the slabs
in their collapsing
geometry completely
realign *graveyard*.
A sea in which the dead are tolling.
Hard earth, perhaps some
roots growing through skeletons.
Small white butterfly by.
The hurricane Vallejo spoke of
in 1924 having shaken the
hospital windows—from
whence did it come he asked,
a patient in its midst.
This graveyard is why Celan
killed himself. All the school
boy order/ardor of death
infinite chessboard where
that certainty of the square,
of the plan—that there *is*
a plan—here gone.
From the 15th to the 18th
century planted. First
burial, the brochure says,
a poet 1439, Abigdor Karo.
How I have depended
upon the school desk
alignment—the plates on
the Thanksgiving table—

the streets, their corners, my
father turning right,
my first date Betty Hartman
and me, a neat box
of space between us,
in the back seat—the order of
that geometrical embarrassment,
of sun conjunct with moon,
the city set in the mind of man,
a jewel in the breath held
wildness of the stone
around which I make my path,
staggered. Sanded by
rain until only Hebrew
script ghosts glow in the gentle
July sun. The sun is not round.
The moon is not a Turkish blade.
The earth is neither round
nor flat but foetus-shaped
like Ogotemmeli said—
and this foetus flying in space
desiring union with a mother
it has yet to conceive, is
also packed in dry dirt,
struck, as with a bomb, by
the history-long climax of death
—which is nowhere.
Unless I pick up more dirt,
more trollops, trolleys, trolls,
the letters lean into each other,
hold me up for support
one slab like a crutch under
its brother—or sister?
Dappled sunlight
on a twiggy thing without leaves
my height.

Prague, 18 July 1976

AT THE TOMB OF ABIGDOR KARO

The Second World War cracked the lid on time,
Pollock's pleistocene scrawls, delight
in his own handprint bloodied
repeat across the canvas wall

—Olson's reach
reaching for
nearly reached ice!
The earth so opened Olson

his shoulder
against paged tombs,
how far back could
he push Pound's wall?

Karo knows how far.
As much life as
was in his death,
the extent to which migraine trust

could be tapped alchemical
bone. A big door. Square and black,
jutting from transistorized ground.
Back through Rouffignac,

mammoth poet,
I know who you are,
myself to the extent I draw
the Sancerre of your tart green

apple out of the spellbound fly-
clustered stucco of lights
under the bat-shaped
density of entrance!

Prague, 18 July 1976

This Doktor Urbanova
her nerve to shake my hand
wagging her head back and forth
so many "I'm sorrys" "You
must excuse mes" meaning
you see I try so hard but
everything, everything is difficult
no one thing can smoothly proceed
—and as I turn to go
"I wish you had not lectured on Mr. Ginsberg."
"I didn't—I did as you asked
me to—a week ago"
"but yesterday I was told
you spoke with some students
about his writing"
"that's right—you did
not ask me not to speak
of him, you asked me not
to lecture on him and in spite of my
strong disagreement with you
I followed your request."
"You see, I'm sorry, but this
may endanger the Summer
Seminar, I'm sorry, but
people told me only yesterday
you, well, ah, went with some
students somewhere and
spoke about Mr. Ginsberg,
you know he was invited here in 1966
and had to, uh, leave the country . . . "

I'm starting to burn,
I ask: "who told you this?"
"I do not feel I am obliged to answer that question."
"So why do you lay
all of this on me at the last minute?
What do you expect me to do about it
right now?" For I had just
said (I now remember 15
minutes later over breadfast)
how moved I had been by
some of the people I had met in Czechoslovakia,
how glad I was that I had come—
it was *then* that she brought up Ginsberg;
the Seminar is not endangered,
the point is not political,
the point is to keep everything a desert,
keep contact and language at desert level
like what does a typical American family
eat for dinner? or, let's sing
folk songs together but let us
not think that the songs we so easily mouth
came originally out of the cannon
soul of black slaves made up
in fields or in latrines—no, keep it all so
boringly superficial no one feels anything.
Urbanova's insulting complaint is not directed against
Ginsberg but to tell me in her cunty way that
she personally resents my having made real
contact with a few students,
that a little water got into the desert,
and such is not Communistic nor Capitalistic
nor Czech nor American—it is
all of them, and none, it
is a condition of character always always present,
keep the blood from flushing out,
hide warmth, channel all energy to officially
determined ends, for the point in talking about any poet

is not dates nor even his meanings, but his
meanings as crowbar to pry open more life.
So *after* Ginsberg discussion one woman
could start to talk with me about her life, the
way she is split between a scientist husband
and another man she loves—
"I have no one to talk about
this with and it is breaking my heart . . . "
Could be in Indianapolis, or Los Angeles,
one wants to generalize at this point so hugely
about human nature, and I collapse on the invisible point,
all explanations are beside the point
the wormy black point human nature
twists or freezes in. Colorfilled.
Colorless.

Prague, 21 July 1976

CHARLES BRIDGE, WEDNESDAY MORNING

So I'll go sit under Christ
across from the attending Marys—
above my head his blackened feet
and before me I can hear a toilet flush
as one of three kiss his still born hand.
Tug horn. A gang of kids curious
   and mischievous about a street painter
   working a riverscape off to my right—
The stroll of morning
   under INRI—last evening
pressed my nose to cathedral doorglass
The magnificence inside! As opposed
   to Prague's present day uncared
      for streets,
packed cathedral, maybe 500 singing
   under gold Baroque ikons, and I thought
they're in there
because they are so unhappy,
Christianity a secondary phenomenon,
the embracing of multitudes rather
   than a single person. The Jesuits say:
"give me a boy until he is 7
and I'll answer for him the rest of his life."
Make a man unhappy and he will be
   comfortable, really, only on his knees
or with his knees on another kneeling person.

Amazing to watch the dark starlings
   lazy 8 the tower spires, a Gothic

weight, anchor of something light
    as breath, up we go, flame,
hang for a second, our selves against
    the double cross of our darker
        Self—then the air clears
      again, Christ an instant
        in the wind

unhappy man wants to rivet there
    eternally mortifying mortality.

Looks as if the riverscape artist has
    a sale. A group of Germans move
    by as if in a barge, glancing
    up at Christ then down at me,
    I think they think I'm drawing—

        Yoroshi desuka? One Japanese
man asks his dapper friend before
clicking the camera. It seems everyone
(but me) is around with a camera,
    they want Christ

with the river behind him *and*
    the "Castle" on the hill beyond.

The river a scaly black, slow, silver
    dull glitterings—black city
with bronze-green onion domes, a yowling
baby is wheeled by fast—

        no purity.   no paradise.

but happiness. What have I been trying
to say about happiness? That it is here,
a part of me, visible, along with
my awareness of so much unhappiness.

93

Say it is the egg in a kind of mix I feel
     daily, once mixed in
impossible to draw the egg out again,
or say it is the muscle that broke
     the chicken leg from its chicken
body when my father could not—

     Note not men but 3 women
lament and kiss the dead Christ—
where are the men?
          they're disciples, or sons—
hanging back, the crowd, the blood
in the feet unconscious as it
     passes through the heart—

If they do love him why didn't they
wrench them away from his *father's* work,
offer him the life in their warm bodies—
and seeing each alone in the crowd
why didn't he go to them and say:
     woman,   animal,   sexual Being,
person,   wife.

     Each morning I kiss Caryl's
photo taken in Devonshire, her
tilted happy face under a bough
lowering a big green apple.
     River odor. Chilly wind.
The semen in the air!
The green appleness in the air!
The semen green translucent density of the air!
The air crutch-filled, free,
     pregnant with stones—

An old man in sandals has just
     stepped in something. How he
          wants it off his heel.

94

Go ahead. Use your hand if you have to, and
smile as it stains, as it gets in
    between flesh and
nail, you nailed man,
son of The Nailed Man, black
    African fetish man, man
with nails sticking from every inch
of his body, barbed, wrapped in bales of it,
with cream-colored gloves dividing
multitudes into hell lines, death lines—

    Both my legs asleep.

    Must be time to go.

Prague, 21 July 1976

AUGUST, SENEX

As the old man
becomes a child again,
he wanders around the house
bumping into the archangelic toys
but they are chair,
edge, they cut his feet,
he bleeds sand,
on the beach he watches
the ankles of his own child
take on no size,
a shiver of anatomy, steady
but quick, sand
yet blood, how
does he nurse this month
through? Does he
take the ocean through
his son shiver?
He is so tired, he licks
the southern California sand,
in the newspaper they say
he is a great stud lion, has fathered
45 cubs at Safari World, eyes
press around
his melting flanks,
he thought to say: I nurse this month,
through 4705 I draw cool earth,
the construction
of this nipple is home
every summer with mother,
her August birthday, the house

candlelit every August day,
lion wax running the walls,
but then he sees something called nostalgia,
he sees how he would like to dress
up the house for this her month,
bridalize the curtains and place
a crescent of ocean outside
the diningroom porthole window,
turn the house into a brideship,
wed his age
to a youth always dividing, always
perhaps double, his childhood
and senexland, where august,
almost regal, the old lion
can only yearn to step back,
paw by paw, into the tiny cub
alcove where he will dream.
The mother wax, when rubbed,
comes off the regal walls of
the imagination, what he presses
against presses back
at him, not a wall, or if
a wall, elastic,
two desperate children, a
shiver and
a living son must make their way
along the beach between
my childhood and my childhood image,
blinding southern sun, the sound
constantly confusing the sun as the son of
a more distant mother? He does not
want to idealize her so
he crumples the ocean creasing
the crescent he probably
cut out at school—to go back to school,
is that why September
is end to this?

Now look here, the ankle
says to its sand,
you are not so simply getting older
but because your age is a part of everything
you age and do not seem to age,
this runs through your fingers,
you cannot quite catch your age because,
since it is sand, and running,
it all seems the same, seems "everything,"
your specific blood.

But before the ocean he has seen that his ankle has
no size, his childhood image thereby widens,
oceanic, word trick,
he swings back into 4705,
twirls through the numbers as if . . .
there is no one to catch him,
mother is neither terminal
nor the force that once projected him,
mother has gone her way,
the curtains, bridally bright, are
stale when crinkled, cake,
the wedding candles might as well
be fence posts, the childhood home
is not even abandoned,
other people live there now,
O if it *were* abandoned he thinks for one
fleeting Tintern Abbey, a mighty ruined
fortress might be his Goddess,
he could place her in it,
an old woman become young,
beaming alternately life death
and if he fucked her there
so that his member
entered earth, would not
the distance between his childhood and
his image of childhood collapse?

Senex and his wandering child
are not much interested in sex,
other than their own navels
which they watch as hourglasses,
sand for senex,
beach for the wandering child . . .

Why don't you call me puer? the child asked,
why child? You still hesitate
before my abundance,
don't you see harvest
lies a month or so behind me
as well as non-verbal sounds,
autumn abundance is always
beckoning, once reached,
like me, the skeleton shows through,
so wise senex knows he does not fray to shiver
but leans a bit to the left
and becomes me again,
ache of first sexual throb,
crutch up into armpit,
the earth, stone-hard
pushing at your vulnerable parts,
don't you see this pain in penetration is
constant sexex pressing against you
threatening to become sentence and go on and on?

The puer had begun to grow little horns,
his body fuzzy, less substantial than when he spoke,
but I recognized now a kind of impatience about him,
had I put him in trousers too early? Blurred,
bothered, he went around in back of the house,
to the backyard, tombstone filled,
on each tomb the name of one
of my grade-school friends?

You see, he began to speak again,

you have said "grow"
as if the branches left the trunk and went
about their business in the sky,
no longer bothered by
the children will always dislike·you.
No matter what you do, or become,
or fail to become, that is your natal
twin and you cannot overwhelm it,
cannot expect your happiness to overgrow
this painful crutch, your walking stick,
what your blindness might very well
learn to use to tap with.
Live in the illusion of growth, if you like,
but also notice its umbrella effect.
August beats through this,
and he to whom I am attached
cares not a whit for your mother memory.

I made my way through the clustered slabs,
around the garage, tapping, no longer looking.
If I looked I knew I would see the senex in Sparkie's dogpen
over my mother, enjoying her amongst the scat.
Keep tapping, something told me,
use this painful
—did he say children? did he mean
the child in others? he said children,
meaning I must live with
the children I knew and their dislike for me?
as it is carried on? I tapped again. The cane end stuck.

So much feeling about September,
this September, song, a blue terrycloth teeshirt
danced against Ann Jones, 1952,
in her Marott Hotel apartment,
"September Song"
                     7th ember, way down in the grate,
the western sun flares in humidity
and the flies, suddenly compelling, cluster
as if witness of
their own meaning,

a fly, a pit
in the sun,
the sun's pit,
its seed

somehow they get into the house, then weakly,
under the weight of their Germanic helmets,
their maggot power so heavy in their arms,
pick their way about the screen, like humans about
ruins, magnetized
                     and the sun licks them off.
Late afternoon today, a dozen pigeons
so ancient against the wide western blaze, their
foil, they might as well have been flies
the high tension wire so loaded by
their clotted bodies,

I wore the darkblue teeshirt again and again,
a good luck charm since the first time I wore it
I felt someone up, in the sun I blacken in that

remembered thing, I am a fly
my paws on the table, ember is the flash
on their helmets, knowing I will never grow again.

"for your father" she said,
and then, "how dedicate a book to
someone who is dead?"
Lavender dusk all over the dining-room windows,
I left making steak tartare, walked out on the porch.
No lavender. All inside. Rose hued,
rhyming with the plum brandy I used in the tartare.
Bach Cantata #93 as we ate. Outside
the royal palm had not been touched,
a cement collar, apartment backed,
pasteled, he is stronger now, an old man
living in this neighborhood—
suppose him across the street,
watching me, thinking about Gladys,
a peculiar tree, he will never rhyme
with another man. Tom Meyer said that when he, Jonathan,
and a third man get into bed,
a fourth as presence seemed to be beside the bed,
then I thought: the denied woman?
a wraith in semen-rags weeping by the post?
I will always put a woman in his place
because he did not seem to want one.
A cap on a ladder chipping paint,
or shoulders over his vise by the furnace.
Other. Did not rhyme with my mother. Or if he did,
the rhyme was so gentle my unmatching hands
would never feel it in substance.
I kneaded the raw meat
and thought about the sparrows in his crown.
Friday night. A disappointing shade—

103

but: he was not a hammer. He did not,
as the men of Idi Amin, force me to pound
a dead man's head to pulp and then put
my head in it for the night. There was no one to kill.
No corpse to be fucked over—
therefore Tantrik stenography is for me unreal?
After Caryl there is only the earth, and
with her once I put myself through her into the earth,
held on to vines for my dear life.
A sunset along the Hudson later, as strange
as this light tonight. But when I went to see him,
at the slaughterhouse, having waited years,
there was only a man at a desk in a large room
with fifty men at desks. This is my son, he said,
to a few of them. Then: well, I guess I'm ready to go.
A few yards away the slaughterhouse
where for years he had walked, on planks I believe,
in his white smock. Mr. Belvedere—
time and motion study. A man watching
a four-way meat clock,
loin chimes, a horn dial,
an animal tick. Nothing got revealed,
nothing was shown, I gather
he was nearly impotent. Why?
When a gang of men tumble into bed
is he the shade by the post?
Blind. With swan's breasts,
perhaps holding a candle, as if
by that light something of the way
people really do things
would become visible?
He is very old and only a small part of him
is in any way mine. My mother noticed that
when she turned over on her side.
Lights out. Crickets. The porch swing still
by the screened morning-glories.
Sure she is asleep, he gets up for a glass of warm water.

Stands by the living-room drapes.
If I could have known for one moment
what he was thinking. About his fire-cracker?
He gave me a hollow
in which to fit, and since I did not,
he fell to ash. Yet never completely.
But one of his clock motions must be called ash.
Bright snow on the lawn. What
was he really thinking? About his cornet?
It is too easy to know. I want to transmit
transformed memory. I want to inhabit
him for a moment, be his figure of woman.
Maybe it is him at Tom's bedpost,
the old man thinking about something like a woman.
That vague. Warmed by the throaty men
he is unsure whether they are fucking or fighting.
They warm him. That is what counts,
no matter that they appear to be flames
and he thinks he stands by the bay window.
No father knows where he is. As long
as he is a father. When he is father, I
am his girlfriend Olive Oil. Cemetery
romance. The American sublime. The men
are coated with snow, he watches the front-
yard writhe, his wife's head in hair-net,
the three men hug and make
an odd pose of her face. He drinks,
as if at a trough. The age tastes of blood.
He is free to walk into the kitchen.
How hungry he is. He peeks into the refrigerator,
it is crammed with alive cattle. He wants
to experience something that is not
father. Father, he says to his own,
pour me a glass of dandelion wine!
And that is the cage. That his father is
locked in too. And the mothers
unawakenable. Why? I have to keep asking.

Why, why, let it press father into
father into ice where only a bison
might be observing. The mothers
are down in the earth with steel in their ears.
The sisters and brothers live even further away.
So why does this father not visit me?
Why does he remain uncertain before men?
Why does he not know that the men in bed
are not hurting one another?
Why doesn't he know they are there
instead of in a cockpit or in uniform?
My father grows older and older by the drapes.
At times I think he has left. Then I creep from my room,
afraid of being scolded,
but since I am older too,
his scold would be a kind of toast.
I knead the meat, unsure of why I am eating it raw.
Was it male too? This is being lost
like I have never allowed him to be before.
An old man necking with himself in a parked car.
A father reaching directly into ice.
Insubstantial. Deer-father the poets cry.
Snail-father. Father in some form.
Why have you become insubstantial
right at the moment deer-woman has thrown off
her fake antlers? Why do you disappear
right as she walks from the deer?
Why are the brothers so far off and why
am I not frightened by the spider I ate?
Why is it so easy to watch a python
brood fifty eggs, why did I see that and not
run alarmed to the nearest bee-hive
dressed up as a ghost to steal their liquor
and rub it all over my body?
Why do I not know why I am here?
On the personal level alone my father turns to me
and then an earthquake turns,

or the moon, he comes and can be viewed.
But the tripod is broken,
the aligator frame is missing.
Meat. Mother's salami made him smile.

Here for the breath of erasure, that's why.

ARCHAI

They came,
my mother and father
were pressed into their vaginal folds,
today they appear to be
the entrance to a cave called Niaux,
they are
what is behind the French Bank on Wilshire Boulevard,
their life
is mixed in what is most present, ephemeral,
and what is behind
being old, a child with several hundred layers of skin;
I can see through the black
parking-lot attendant reading Frank Yerby,
in the spine is Aimé Césaire
and if we could open Césaire full circle
would an animal clock face appear,
could my age be told
by the amount of centuries in my chimes,
by what has run down
through my eyes into my lees,
my wine cellar, where my mother and father
still alive grow until they are opened—
if as a wound they will evaporate,
if as Caryl a dream increases in my flesh,
the dream of a cave where the animal visions are
enchased in stone the grandparents of stained
cathedral glass. They made the cave,
before them the earth
was compact, a looking-glass, unenterable.
They saw through their reflection,

they gnawed the dust mirror, slowly
they began to climb into their skeletons,
a warship, a place of worship, words
then were two feet thick
like the walls of the Staronova Synagogue in Prague,
windows were hesitant,
narrow and deep-set eyes,
rainbow was what they did,
what fell through them
bubbled on the floor—if there was a floor—
sometimes there was ocean
sometimes there was origin,
a dark red soundless glare,
orgasm was the morning hiked
and behind aurora's veil
the sprint of maggots felt like a splint,
something strong, thin, a kind of wince
that could be bound to pain,
levels of pain were compost
and they actually fucked where they sowed,
Death had not yet disappeared
so in its house they spent their afternoons,
its structure was sunset
wholly carnivorous, eating flora
as night's mouth closed, vaginal-anal,
virginal, fresh. I see them
at times in the double eyes in chance
or in the woodwork, or in flowers,
or in clouds, or in anything
that does not seem to intend seeing.
What did they do? They came,
with the most elaborate head-dresses,
their minds trailed behind them nearly
to the ground, their minds
were braided so they could braid
the manes of the powers, thunder
and lice, or open sore

and sor-row, the Noh
ghost hears them at times repeating
wot
his
sor
row.
But then rows away, a wave-man like us,
endless, prolegomenon.

FOR JAN BENDA

Suppose the word no longer holds
water, can it be used as a drum?
Listen to him beat it today, Sinatra
slumped at the base of a well
his sombrero over his eyes
asleep? Of course, but
not to the thousands of
helmeted lizards who
fill the desert—they feel
his words hold water, they
do not hear the dry tock of each word
as a piano-tuner hammer
breaks it like a walnut shell.
A drum. They feel it's his heart or
is it a stranger than night
heart beat? A head
wrapped in a muffler over
wound bandages, perhaps the waiter
on which Sinatra broke
a full ketchup bottle in
his lived life-like life.
So "heart" is beat, "love"
is beat, "you" is leeched
leaving the letter "u" as remains,
and the person who says his own experience,
who is umbilical to his word,
appears to be a baby still
connected, as if
still-born. "Cut him loose!"
something under

mind cries, "it's death to be
connected still, once outside,
to the force that nourished us
while we were inside,
cannibal, wrapped in water."
Outside? At times I am word prone,
yoked to a kind of tubing
ending in insect feelers, a wet
nursed by an orange
nipple grazing in my palm,
I see through a veil of rain
—at times. But then it's as if I doubly
awake, and the language withdraws into
doubled sleep, Pancho
Sinatra, curled up,
a husk under the starlight
imprinted ón the mind
like a player-piano roll.
It is so obvious and
it is the source of despair everywhere.
But who cares when care can be done for you
by a mouth caramelized duhdum.

JALAPA

A queen is an emphasis,
robed in gilt, which Caryl
has released, leaving me
hollow by her side, her arm
the bone
pain deposited, the flesh
soft, loose,
the bone livid.
How might she rule
these distracted areas?
I set my hollow
by her pain,
jalapa, for aching
in arms and legs,
hollowpain,
jalapa, from Nahuatl
Xalapan, "sand in the water"
the town where it
was first obtained
through the compassionate
vision of an angel
queen who assimilated
an ancient rite;
the sorceress was held
by the men over
a basket, the snake
knew where to go
to make her scream,
from her cries they
sublimated language,

"serpent power"
they said, "is now
within us, lies
curled at the base of
our spines; we must
meditate it up to
see its peacock cobra hood
in our own eyes."
Over this rite
the Nahuatl angel
queen set a pan of
ground jalapa root,
"let those men
eat of this image"
she said, "their sublimation
is based on torture,
thus no human
good can come of it.
I will use
their act and sublimation
as fuel to purify my root,
jalapa,
'sand in the water,'
hand in the lava, emerge,
massage."

THE WOOD OF ISIS

I cling to her chest, as if
from a spring, rising and falling,
as if from "the great mother"
as if there were still
enough power in "as if" to
carry me, a monkey on
her lapel—to think of you
now involves a "her"
in parenthesis, she is a word
coming back into human language,
not the cooperating Isis
but the wood of Isis,
the trunk of word
in which a dismembered
"would" begins to laugh
at the mummy with the long
member, Isis
in back of Caryl,
you are, bound fast,
still breathing life back into
my "cult phallus" the piece
of cedar they attached to
the man made
out of death, everlasting
man, who goes up in fire
every time bread is suffered,
broken, older than
father a great mother
yawns, aurora
starts to replace dawn

or is the sensation
my desire to say
what you, Caryl, mean?
Something is being doubled,
perhaps the great mother
has found a mirror
and sees a Caryl
through my word,
shattering the witch
who meditated in the cracks of
Snow White, perhaps two
children lost in the web
of a Disney comic
have started to feel
the African child only
a few inches
under Christmas, under
underwear, their albino
playmate who is hidden in fog,
or is it all
to be swept away, Dutch
Cleanser, brume,
the language so fractured
that what I travel on
is a road without camino,
a Spanish word without
its Japanese dō,
a stepping down without
the sense of person, not
as someone to be stepped
on, but as the sense
in object that offers gender;
the old great mother is so
banished that an end
appears to be assembling,
man's "everlastingness"
is now clearly his impotence to be

origin and to account
for his desire to be made of steel,
as if all guns were cloth,
but none of them are, no
rich man is going to release
his poor man, no priest
is going to break down
the wood between
his confessional's ears.
I think about what you mean
before a glass of wine
in which the intoxication is
very old, before a pheasant
in which the grain
is so young that I almost
fail to see their fermentational
cross of which the Christian
cross is but an awkward sign.
Isis, your wood
is the verde that pulls
under the Spanish, not alone
in my heart, but as if
under my heart
in place of organs
there were a hollow child,
a grotto, a mouth
gasping between the edge of ozone and
infinity—if I could just
give birth! But I cannot,
and I know this as a wall
trapped between a man and the bed;
the end now has three sides,
one can tell the time by an animal's face,
incest is hardly a knob,
primavera is lying down,
to assimilate what I feel
means to cease anticipating

a wholeness before any act,
"boke ole mamma
getta new mamma"
Isis, stop cooperating
with the moment's
unending male inauguration
yet do not assume
behind that first sentence
there is a time that were we
to stop packing the air
with death and God
could be matriarchal
adventure; I see you
impacted in my mother's
father's death
where he was automobile
and train but none of the passengers.
Man is a collision
in which all that he has engineered
signals red glass, black glass,
whirring coral snake I come from to go.

CORE MEANDER

I sit here, sinking, shipwreck
most desired, infinite where
beech boughs hold
red and gold chariots,
the drivers and all the riders;
it is 3 AM, in the dream I
could not get home by subway,
a wrong direction took me not merely to
the next stop but over chasms
through a forest where I beheld
the beeched chariots, the passengers
happy although the road
appeared to be below them forever;
I figure in a sun spoke stroking
Caryl, partially stone we are disfigured
toys, "how did two little goobies
like us get together?"
Having recovered from our lives,
enlaced in our spoke
still turning, beached or
high in the dream beech, the fraternity
guile has fled, although rings of
where I stand show
decaying growth
worked into imagination,
which is not hateful, as Antin
has recently said, but anti-
transcendental work, drilling through
given dream to recreated dream;

below me, the road which grips
the knees of many I seem at moments
above, only in imagination
am I free, in stomach I too am
on my knees before an altar
where not even a message has been left;
I inch my way outside convinced
that everyone can stand, knowing
most leave the earth
unloved, my biology reaches
a red stone temple behind
the cathedral where it knows
it will be healed, there Isis
with Caryl strapped to her back
receives my bones and blood,
she breaks my word into
violets, it is not violent
where I am, a squid countess
is shuffling my pain into
the deck of her face;
to make my word hold
where I am not must also
enter and be held,
the poetry in which I stand is chard
and tinder, archangelic toy
underslung with tubs of
asylum gruel at Artaud o'clock,
focused on what Caryl means,
petrified, two figures at times only
arms, Caryl and Isis exchanging backs,
at once the structure and
the specific person, his d stem
broken God looks like Goo,
the second o is redundant,
I adhere to Go, a baby
curled about his mamma's waist,
her serpent ally, she is the sun,

her armbeams toss me high,
I'm her little eel, diaphanous
in her light, core meander
a hominid guards by
gashing out branches from the line,
bristlecone pine my dream
hones and reshapes,
the Indianapolis balloon man on the Meridian
Street bridge appears,
we stop, it is exactly noon,
the balance absurd, the absurdity
balanced: Ira liked to hear him say
"fiffeen chench."

FOR MILENA VODICKOVA

What do you
mean by "happy"
Milena asked.
I punctured a hole
in Donald Duck, Pollock's
"The Deep" showed
the cenote
under Duckburg,
Donald and his nephews were
diving for Mayan treasure,
an Indian kid
reading a Disney comic
was slowly being absorbed,
the Ducks were swimming
through stagnant
mind, the kid looked
behind him, the comic closed—
he was on a nice sofa, yellow wall,
green grass outside, he wandered
down the barriada road dazed
by the Disney construction,
people were shouting, Indian
laborers were carrying signs,
"There's a thirsty looking group!"
Donald cried, "Hey, people,
throw down your banners and have
free lemonades!" coins spilled
from his glove, "A tall cool one,
merchants!" one demonstrator cried,
and another: "I'll have one here *and*

one for the road!" The Indian kid
was thirsty too, even though the air
seemed folded with water,
the stench from the barriada
pump where his mother washed;
Donald brought up a treasure-trove
and started to jabber to his nephews:
"These idols stand
for the Indian mind," Dorfman & Mattelart
translated, "once our adventure
is produced, and in some Indian
kid's hands, it
will be his wealth and we
his North American friends."
Milena's question
gets me, because
with Caryl not here, us
lacks the coherence of I love and
am loved, it includes
not only the South American I exploit
but Milena herself, the manikin
of a Russian soldier in the shop window
of her Czechoslovakian
breast, her heart
manikin-occupied,
a Russian dressmaker
at work with his palms—
in South America the soldiermaker
is soldered to hunger;
I must face my personal happiness
with that Indian
kid, I thought,
again the language
turned inside out,
my happiness is
faced with him like a building
faced with marble,

[*How To Read
Donald Duck*,
International
General, NY,
1975]

his energy
decorates me,
what I am is finished with his façade.

HEARING BETTY CARTER

Is she formed around her mouth?
Is her mouth a well rim,
a birth bath she is raising to the sun?
Dogon granny chewing blue dirt.

Under her lower lip
the skin, for an instant,
inflates, "Blue Moon"
a lizard balloon.

She plays with on
with in, with us,
scourging the white
clothes from "Blue Moon."

Grounded, om
holifies, a note
goes into withdrawal,
she drawls

then rat faces the sound,
her soprano
lilt crumbles into
bass molasses,

fresh water
in the stale bird bath of lyric
into which she drains
her angel, wrings out

the discs of grease
the bitter angel is
slipping into her mouth,
"what mortal brace can do"

"hot to conceive it"
scat wandering on a chain,
as if a line could be
articulate in night.

Real questions behind the language
bars, buried within scat
she tries to swing through the bars,
turns into plastic woman

"withouta looka my own babe"
belongs to no one
who believes in nothing,
now a citadel

in which energetic no one
pants with cliché, a negative
become a contour, active,
a black hole in person

where nothing is lost,
takes root, grows and projects,
Aztec speech-scrolls,
flames, faces with blowtorches of nothing

against the twisted
old master frame, the painting has dropped out
the struggle
to guard her enlarged om vessel.

AFTER THE SECOND DEATH

the death of both mother and father,
an other begins to compose itself,
teramorphous bone,
tomb and muscle of their embryos—

I sensed it in my face
driving away from the second burial,
the full corps of pistons which drive
the embryo corpse machine was activated,
I was my face in my car,
my vehicle of mental travel had been
contraried out, a rented Pinto.

Today, 6 years later, I see that other
fold, an eyed fist, into itself
and stream away, inside out, leaving a ragged
hole, as clouds tear to sun, in that
hammock which has one end tied to embryo,
the other to corpse—a hammock
because those twin ties turn life's
vertical into a place of lassitude,
they add the crossbeam to
the vertical man, and his psychology is
slung, embryo tie at head,
corpse tie at foot, in
the distance of the freshness of childhood snow from
his hanging belly—

he cups his girth and feels, as if
at the end of his mind, a sparkle of snow,

128

he feels its perfume of air and future life
through an odorless width,
his flesh becomes the distance
between that snow and present life—

at this point, the witch is born, hag
riding his impotence, her prune face,
his balls, audacious orchids, all
gather into the rapidly building teratoma.

FOO TO THE INFINITE

"Play vanilla," Lester Young is said
to have said to a piano player
comping too elaborately behind his solo . . .
but I like your noise
in here with my own,
but how much? How much
anything in here with my
own? How is that true? My "own"
is only the hue of ruddy purple
on the otherwise black
massed segments of a fly's eye—
which may be more
sun accompaniment than
what I generate. What do I generate?
A swath through front walk snow,
at least a place for me to walk, and
you too, if you come out
before the god of snow,
neither hostile nor loving,
dumps again. A place for your feet,
a kind of box to walk in,
a kind of end that goes on
50 feet before turning to lice—
I propped an l against i.c.e,
so as to not come to conclusion here,
Ira Clayton Eshleman,
but the play has started up, I mean
the play called Foo To The Infinite—
until now, I realize, I had been off stage
glittering with the thought of thinking I was on.

That was because the other side could not be seen.
But now it is happening, and the audience
—I think there is one out there—has brought its lunch
—yes, there he is—my father
eating the skeleton of a hamburger
motions "You want some too?"
Play vanilla, I say to him, and he to me: "play dead."

STILL-LIFE, WITH AFRICAN VIOLETS

The little pot of them in the Beverly
Hills flower shop window,
purple sable, sand, African
violence, a crazed very black
man shouting at the flower shop,
Africa pulled up to within feet of
Beverly Drive, he shouts from sand and luster, sweating,
but from the flower shop he just moves his mouth, he is dirty,
hysterical, he is waving a hoe, the clerks
glance at the window sometimes, a siren or
customer's nose presses against
the African violets on their mind,
nothing moves, begins to squirm
between the hoarse African and the neat lady clerk,
nothing finally starts to move, the air
so packed with everything the African has neglected to do,
the lady clerk looks down at
the straw in her soda, thinks of God, how silly, sucks
at the frothy bottom, the African rolls over on his mat,
the pain in his anus will hardly let him hoe, the night is not
death rich with the transformational mesh of sky and field,
but skinny with death, white goons in jeeps drip
from his brow, he picks up a handful of dust,
nostalgic gesture, the lady clerk is nostalgic gesture,
if they were both smeared on a rock he
would be denser, she would be mucilage, a bird
would stay by his smear longer, nothing thinks
this is very funny, that part of my mind touched by nothing,
soft frayed earlaps of violets,
nothing surrounds them, crushes them when it throws a fit,

yet since all of us are in social time
I will not try to balance myself on nothing,
I will believe the enraged African is thicker
than the Beverly Hills lady clerk, in doing so I will betray
my own life a block south of Beverly Hills,
my physical body is here with the retail violet instead of with
the violet in the earth; I want him to smash the jeep goon,
but I better be ready to deal with the black man when he
kills the goons, especially when I saw one of their white hands,
just a second ago, come in the window and take hold of my left wrist,
I shook it off with a chill, a floral chill, the embroidery of a fangy
white African hand with purple veins touched my wrist to caution
    me
No way to take sides and to think at the same time,
you either allow both that black and that clerk to be in contradiction
or you pass into a thinness, your word must be
at least as thick with sand and sable, dry animal
tongue out, the terrified goon's neck cradled,
sliced, desperate lizard, fly trapped between screen and window,
say "African violet" and Pandora begins to twitch with her goat feet,
the mutiny that tickles nothing begins to stir and then yawns before
your corrected feelings . . . So is the point to strengthen
the glass between us to the point that nothing feels pinched
and begins to abandon us? How? By a good deed? By sweating in our
imaginations? By breaking up the altar glass near the end
of our minds, where the religious explanations sit
attentive and foreveresque in blue uniforms with gunpowder-braid?
How does an African with a hoe do that? He hits a tree, he
hits his kid, I mentalize a terrifying lode of world in Beverly Hills
African violets, but our acts are not the same, Oh yes they are
Pan squeaks from the molecule in which he is trapped, the atmos-
    phere is
now so packed with nothing there is no real difference between a slap
and a wince of perception, an animal starts down a dusty glass path,
think of her as a tear running a flower shop window or as a disease
shaped like a cougar boiling with a craze for release,
you will only yoke this beast by traveling as a tear in these other

wills, you will need the protection a tear ball can give you,
a head, feeling the outpack of the air, striations of nothing like
    gossamer
red veins in the air, pull them down and that fancy white hand will
    again
clutch at your arm, lucky man, leave them be and the same force may
maggot your width, you are where repetition is parallel to itself,
clutch-clutch, meaning Animal why don't you get to where you are
    going,
you, animal, you, black cougar with lady clerk spectacles, you, fly
with paws, boiling to release nothing, to see the extent of the silage
in the depths of nothing, a compost or billions of howling beings?
You got a wink of them at Hiroshima and you actually touched
your portion of their skin at Yunotsu, you sat in green mineral
water in which the hives of burning were large as frogs, now
break in hell as well as heaven, see them in goosestep before your
    eyes,
fly which is a cougar suffering, eating its hoe behind the rich people's
flower shop, an inch behind your head, where you dwell with
    Sammy
Davis Jr., in the same porcelain cup poised on the descendingly
    atrocious
ant-hill-like living strata suckled by that meek mold, nothing.

THE NAME ENCANYONED RIVER

Hello and farewell, César Vallejo, at the margin of
your name encanyoned river, complete,
yet utterly rushing away, the bottom is dry
and in motion, enchased, liquor
pounding at its casket sides, buried treasure
half afloat in sand, translating is a child's
game, there is nothing in that ornate chest,
pirates are stumps set on quicksand,
translating is a man's name, pirates are rapists,
the cabin shudder emits its Dachau
oven whistle, what is inside the name?
For fifteen years you have rivered my sleep,
as if I slept under your gun,
as if my dreams took place in the pipe
you flowed through, language
can weigh you, tell how much you are
other, how much you were
ego, you flow dust
between Indian presence and Catholic presence,
a Marxist conundrum, the heir is endless
as well as the variations on what I can see, a text
is a staircase leading down into a vault
where a man with a face like a turnip explains
through teeth knotted gums that he is neither coward
nor hero, neither the king I expected to find in my tomb
nor the slave I passed in the toilet, but a composition
I was redoing out of my desire to realize
another, happened to be called César Vallejo,
leaving tracks I followed, in deepest
sincerity, around the stone

now articulate in Caryl's gaze,
which then disappears down the gullet of the dead-snake gnawer,
alone in the flesh vale, beyond the lights of the carnival,
that groin we met in, anxiety
over the weight of the infant cowl in each dawn
and the elderly scrawl in each sunset, a penis with
its chicken head shot off. You were to sleep in my dream
when my urge was blocked by maggots,
you appeared a dead hobo between Barbara and myself,
your marble face insapphired crystal,
a river frozen between ego and other
my senses could not thaw
until I wept into you, got my tears in hand,
a cry for the infant of occasion to break
through the back turned linoleum of the hardened present
world, as if the discussion were *What shall we eat*
and took place in the kitchen, instead of *Why most do not*
which churns in the thyroid of television,
life is up to you, they say, and how you feel
cutting up a TV set for dinner, a problem of translation,
the Vietnamese peasant whose blown apart head,
dots on the screen, still disengages, verbs, adjectives,
pieces of linkage of cosmic creatures,
irreflective puddles at the foot of a shattered tree,
the lager is despair, pools which lie around each
turn of mind "but you knew it was self-reflection,
so why did you expect a bridge?"
That voice—from where does it come?
From the reader, of course, in a plane,
a concerned academic friend, who glimpses me below
tangled in the landing-gear, covered with Entebbe or some other
horrible occasion, death as the ground of inspiration
but so far below and so total, I fly with talons in my back
while my feet stroll on a ball-bearinged earth.
Dragged from soil to soil each person knows,
if only at near orgasm, archeological strata is the dirty
gossip, the obscene penetration. Nature and God

136

tunnel us, stone smoothing gadgets, our value
increases as the edges become more porous,
again I am inside The Temple of Inscriptions,
dazzled by the ornate sarcophagus lid,
"The grandeur is all back there!" it shouts,
muffled by the heat of the jungle around us,
"And all here!" the skeleton beginning to breathe
between the tall neighboring trunks
rubs and whines. In the back drawer of the imagination and
the frontal narrowness of perception
I went to your wall, I gave it drink,
the wail drank, the wall opened its mouth
stone, then split, its gullet shone like mink,
I am the mother crying a chain to
the daughter behind bars, you are the grandfather
in whose hand suffering is softness untranslated,
the steel muck between the text and the poet's
desire to know what his sex
wants to inhabit, who fears the air of what
he has seen, who tears apart his own tears
to know the minute monolithic weight of the mists,
his fathers, swirling towards him, as if he owed
them anything, for they are his compost
that has suddenly had the nerve to speak!
Our pores are full in each bud, each
a little bath speared by the air, they
deepen yoked to the soft yellow they sag in,
they bud and age, oppressed and enlivened by
multivarious influences, anxiety
was the base until the ego recoiled on its stem against
its hood, until it spread its hood and released
the Korean laborers from the furnace of Japan!
Connection and correspondence must be allowed to
abide, kill, mutate and progress,
organs die and revivify, die
and misdirect, through the glass-bottomed text
your opaqueness still swims,

daddy-long-legs sport in the topsoil and the critic
is a condition of not enough poetry
heard when the parents are evaluated,
my writing is air-conditioned over
the breasts of Beverly Hills anxieties,
Jesus mounted on Darwin's turtle, on whose shell is written:
hello and farewell, rib of Kyoto, on which the core
meander was not Bashō but Vallejo, slug
which finding himself at the bottom of the kitchen sink,
late at night, disappeared back through the drain,
worked his way through the maze of the Cross to
the roots of the figtree to climb its trunk and be seen,
in morning sunlight, motionless on the stump
of a hacked off branch. At the point in the imagination
where an answer is begged for,
there is sweat, ikons belong to the religious,
my joy in the literal was to believe in you,
not misuse you as my own blocked worksheet,
but notice the sit crease at first, as I stood up
and you were left, a transfusion took place,
seat, you held—when I reflected,
you were resistance, or the crawling
desire to have done with the difficulty of
keeping the light on and letting the stars in,
"Greatness" wears cream-colored gloves
and checks the hands of those who pass by it,
living behind a veil and operating as the manipulator
of human fear, a figure whose imagination has become
a closet stacked with ikonic mirrors. My grandfather was
killed in the collision of stoppings,
no more grandfather, just parents and children,
no more grandfather, just our dreams of connections,
no more grandmother, just the train signals,
no more grandmotherfather, just the slide into the micro-oven
so that man curses himself and dreams his penis ogre,
his very breath spotted; the poet takes this error,
traces it back to its source of other,

where there is never A solution, but pores
opened for one person which would be asphalt
for another, the fault of the ass
should be a joke by now, but as the grandfather
webs over, the other is increasingly
mistranslated as machine, the anal levers give
up and people increasingly crowd their right
eyebrow with their left, an unnatural dimple occurs,
the fat over one socket begins to push the straight-forwardness
of the other, for the other is the most inhuman, is the gap
in which the teratoma finds a voice, victim scrawling
its body along the curb, at 10 years old, refusing to smell
the bread baking, there is a lark flying over a French hunter,
there is a cave in which the skeleton of paleolithic tension
is a pack of tiny red spiders running around on a stone,
the apprentice contacts a realized other,
he has a choice to encircle or
to glue himself to the other's mirror,
the other, when first contacted,
turns his back a wall of stone,
the apprentice scratches red dots,
signs of menstrually blessed vegetable patches,
his Cro-Magnon torque to be in history:
mirror me, but double the mirror,
mirror my actual reflection but steam what I am
with the lie of myself I seek to erase,
give me the bread of your tensions, not their crusts,
for I am a greedy pig converting your table into a trough,
the apprentice must demand and demand and demand, not
of the outward man, but the ticks and
the worms of which what is mastered is composed,
crowned ticks and worms in long queenly gowns that were,
in the process of being mastered, crumbling bark and loam,
stuff that appears to endlessly repeat itself, a handful of weeds
or moments of desire which in their infinitely complex nature
appear to be minute cathedrals in which sea-urchins are worship-
    ping,

where wolves are handling The Book of Psalms, moments in which
the freedom of movement wears a lush religious gown,
and this gown when looked at carefully is composed of one-eyed
     jacks,
and then of black and white rags, and finally of bare kneelings,
the poor before a Jesus candle while the switches of the parents
swing through the censorial smoke, these are the moments when
     desire
if not confronted encloses the apprentice in a diving-bell,
the back of the master may still be at work in the flood
but the diving-bell rolls free and becomes a beautifully curtained
     cage,
a stage-coach of sorts in which the aged apprentice is riding,
a grandfather clock ticks away before him in his compartment,
its ornate face is closed, a lid of sorts over a mechanism
that magnetizes the past in all things, trees flash by and he
thinks of a childhood night walk with a flashlight he had shone up a
     trunk,
he failed to puncture himself, he did not escape Aladdin's fate,
he is no longer an apprentice, yet he is, a guest in the backward
reflecting bottle-shape of poetry, an aging homunculus hearing
in each clippity-clop the om-coated mice by his own bitter toes.
Vallejo, in my simultaneous farewellello, the split-level
existence, the male poet caught between mush and glass, was
shattered; facing the height of your contradiction I tore the moss
out of the kingly sockets of The Temple of Inscriptions, from
     moment to
moment I stand in the socket itself and see the socket for what it is,
a butterfly socket, a basin of stone, again and again I must erase
this central mirror, the closet I experience in living
in which I seek to put on my mother's girdle
and appear a likable goy before my friends,
the closet in which I put on my friends' lies
and seek to appear an appropriate bride for my father!
Concentrated by your flesh, I transferred my inner gold to

my surface iron, I saw the task was to live in the amplitude
of contradiction, not in the deathhouse of male versus female
desire; "parasite" is now clear: the poet
must grip into his own caterpillar,
as the caterpillar he must expel his digger-wasp,
his White Anglo night crawler which slips
between his sheets, slyly asking for mercy
while it deposits ikons in all his inkwells.
Still vital in poetry is the belief that the master can
keep his back turned and his vulnerability present,
that the apprentice will have the strength
to reflect that back until he gives himself mind.
This is why a person should want to live,
not to break oneself into children, but,
off the back of one's chosen backing,
to become a mirror, absorb, break, and be porous,
then assimilate the mirror one has chosen, hold
the essence of reflection,
as long as one can, then shake that dear
prey, once one's master, once big as the world,
out of one's fingers . . .
You were the deadest, César, of all
the teen-age dance class, you were the most ugly,
your breath most rancid graham-crackers,
you alone were transplant
to that place that at 13 years old I could only sense,
the wall, the force of your flower, I desired to dance
with a duplication of my duped unknown soul, you
would not back me, your blemishes eased me again and again
around the marble corners of an uncomplicated face,
I allowed my repulsion of her breath, anygirl's,
to hold for several weeks and as I did what was rancid
yielded the excavation inherent in each breath brick,
weightless, I made underwater strokes, the elderly sunfish
glowed black at me, there was a touch of race but mainly

the laced across streets collapsing in soft bags and slick
black shoes, a frame was being built of our elbows and horizontal
arm holdings, we were frames into which we were to spend the rest
of our lives finding the picture that would agree with the way
our left arm was jacked up, the grips of puberty accumulate,
they are the gears of the poems one writes up to 35 or 40,
at the same time these grips amass, a wall, anyone can
scramble over, but to drill through? Why, in drilling through
my own wall must I attach myself to another's back?
Where does such terrifying magic come from?
That my own obscurities are not enough, that I must deepen
and perplex them, that unable to understand the trunk
I must assume nothing about the roots, there may not be
a beginning, or an end, yet every child experiences
the underhim kissing him, that horrible embarrassment!
Personal is released from confessional ties,
the conspiracy in world poetry against a person
openly and imaginatively working with what has happened to him
is the terror of the fathers, what I felt muted
in the overgrown vacant lot next to 4705,
the soft stomach of the poem
made to believe that its navel is vile;
personal is not private, person is what accrues to me,
the personal is a volatile exchange, the nose of the fish
and its gills as well, I only really advance open and eaten by
what passes into/out of me, I am the poem with a focus
disturbed yet happy with my pilot fish, ancient Cross
is to say its arms out and head on, to endure the tension of
puberty not as a mantle but as the eye at the end of the vault
in which a cherry tree is blooming, zero is a lasso this tree knows,
each of its jade and pink blossoms is aglow with nature and
with God, cradling its river, encanyoning lingam and yoni,
not as ikons but as flexions, the process known as Vallejo
insapphires and unties the glistening hocker
of Indiana, scrawled on a diner toilet wall:

"A little bird with golden bill / perched upon my windowsill;
I fed him crumb and crust of bread / then smashed his fucking
    head."
Hail and farewell, César Vallejo, I collect this gravel
from the plate glass of your back, I am your widower,
dearest created brother, until the healthy legs
are surrounded by the resurrection of the lame.

SATANAS

I

Those old fucks won't back me, they offer an elf's condom, saying: here's an awl—penetrate sausage. As if I had a board to eat, a plank from Plato's forehead, even a splinter of my friend Svetla, now gone down Charisma River, lit by rock stars, covered by the graveyard of Ophelia's galoshes . . .

Still, the crowds gather; they want to be titilated by some blue, some bright blue in the blackness. Reap the om ires, learning—I tell'm, but it's those old fucks who arrange the chairs, stir the batter, arouse even the stars they think. Between me and those old fucks stands a cave bears used for crib and burial, for belly rubs, for Dodgem. Old fucks young fucks, no difference between a sopping spore and an elf's condom, the layers between claw and muzzle fuse and the sabre-tooth tiger, punctured and padlocked, starves before his moose feast . . .

I see a bunch of rich medieval Italians supping in a forest, waited on by gnomes, wine and venison deck the silken cloth, it is dusk and even the terrible smell of their collective breaths is not hinted at. They sit deep in the mind of a California apartment, like a well of infinite blue water, as if the pastel prefabricated walls could descend and sup, as if that forest were Chambertin in each leaf and shadow. Those old fucks are there, well behind the table, noting in their ledgers the necessity to at least send a post-card of the voyage back to North Durham or Cambridge, they pull at their hose and breeches, aware that each sag is a little death, each wrinkle a post coitus tristum—but they scribble on, of course, after all, they seem to own the forest as well as war and peace, one look of approval and the suppers will slide from their chairs and hasten to their mounts, driving their wives before them, well-saddled upon their hounds.

144

And who will they fight, you may very well ask? The very horse they chase! The horse that only last night filled their eyes with visions of bleeding stables and lavendar dusks, for the point of all war, is it not, is to dress up in the prey and prance like the King o' May—the victim's skin may still be wet as that of a flayed prom-queen but the leaves do burgeon, and that is the point, to keep the table well-fed, the dirty knives and forks watered, the rooms heaped with dead foliage and the fireplace lit with goldfish . . .

But those old fucks may be torn from their ledgers by the piercing cry of their own maidenheads in distress! Much more possible than you think, for a wrinkle or even a buckle may begin to dream its own liberation, and something odd as a truffle start up as the hemorrhoid of an oak root heretofore suppressed by the forest—I mean, if those old fucks won't back me I may, in revising my strategy, become a verbal timber moving rapidly toward the feast and lawnmower the pressure they seem to be exerting on my rear—for being middle-aged, thus medieval in the scale of history, with the weight of the totality of condoms a constant threat of cave-in on my back, of me, of the sailor-cap and African sandals I have fairly won in my fight to pass in one door and, keeping within the same room, pass out by another door, a brief flight, true, all too brief if one conceives of oneself as a swallow which having entered a drawing-room has one fast spin before another window intercedes on behalf of its only true competitor: death—and now you see why those old fucks treat me as they do, for I must appear as a drawing of a swallow on the wall they pass by rapidly, knowing the interceding window is near, a swallow, neither female nor male, but apodictic, adopting the posture of indifference, out of which I must sculpt my acts into invented hostility and love. Thus I take on size, a size that perhaps exceeds me, I project a size greater than what I feel I am, like the Noh dancer moving swiftly yet slowly across the stage, diagonally increasing in height as he moves to suddenly loom a giant image before our eyes! An apparition, of course, in the sense that the Italian suppers are, and those old fucks? Of them I am less sure. At times they seem to be the mid-point between ceiling and floor, or the frost in any sunny day, quite possibly the day's rudder as well as its helm, and perhaps even the hand which turning the compass regulates the cardinal roses

with sex as death . . .

II

Of course. I think those words a lot, meaning something more
than "of course," the longing to be on course. To think that when I
say "of course" I am of my own curse, in course, corsical? Corsetted?
Perhaps I have been given a cornet, something nostalgic in me lies,
for the truth is my father's cornet renews my desire to trumpet. I
came back into this narrative because I began to feel that too much
had been made of those old fucks. There they are, dressed up like
Ben Franklin, at the edge of that luscious medieval clearing, safe,
back in the Chambertin of the forest. Why do I focus on them instead
of my vision of the feast? Well, that is the problem of growing up—if
those old fucks mean anything at all. Between them and the feast is
the word "nature" on crutches, stalemated between vine and ego,
just "nature," chipmunks, bees, the carnivorous swarm of dryness
and pullulation. Since I have been imprisoned here, my hunch has
been that those old fucks are responsible for my being unable to leave
what I have referred to as my middle-age. When I force myself out of
the angelic space of my spirit I find myself in what is called the
medieval age. No particular time. But in a very particular context. I
find myself in a choir of caterpillars, strong green bodies lifted up
from a leaf pavilion, in a rushed intense light of woods and souls, and
I hear a constant hallelujah—of sorts. For one like myself, to find
myself among caterpillars is to feel intensified what I felt before
intuitively—middle-age, medieval age. For is not the caterpillar
medieval to origin and completion? Therefore it is weird to feel the
cathedral leave, and to stand at a further remove from those old
fucks, in a kind of echeloned "nature," at a staged remove, from the
feast I wanted to see go on, those old fucks noting special things
about a footnote as it pulled at them or as they found deposits in their
coitus tristums, myself in a kind of choirloft with my own kind, not a
safe place, wooden, dark, softened by candles and prayer, but a
dozen of us out on a leaf at the very edge of the language, facing our
destiny as if through a telescope, at first through those old fucks and

146

then through the increasingly distant Italians, surfeited, collapsing into the cloth, in spite of the tremendous forestrial height above them . . .

My tendency so far seems to be to apologize, thus to be forever a son. If you are a careful reader, I imagine that you have suspected that I am a kind of eternal son eternally at war with an eternal father. The species that is willing to play the son long after it has ceased to operate as a son because it suspects what is merely adult. I squat behind those old fucks as if we were in a beauty parlor, they are having their nails worked on, and as their hardness is briefly eased their dreams appear tiny bubbles on their lips. I need to see that I am not cooperating with the figures in their bubbles, for there is a drawing-room in their relaxation where I could be seduced and backed, and that would mean that I had become the scholar of an invisible poet. They would back me if I was willing to imagine the poetry of their youth, if I were willing to conceive the burnt-out armature of what once was the fern in the swept storm of their puberties and present it as a timidly glowing hell. This is why my face is inspissate, hard, heraldic.

What a tremendous desire to have done with those old fucks! Such a desire that I have lost them and returned to them, as if out of nostalgia—for as they are archai they are also parents, and as I am mortal I likewise have my diamond armature; such a parallel suggests that the total number of childhood dinners is thicker and has more to do with diamond than with any object—or objective. The archai are soft as smoke, but the actual fathers are the torsion between the vise and what it holds. From the false beginning of history grandfather after grandfather is a crib, by such thatch the infant is given grain even while he gurgles and plays!

Each night, creation, caught red-handed in the act of itself, is repeated.

III

I am always finding and losing, as a clock hand swings, between back and forth, between the extremes that a sense of foetus and

147

corpse lead me to believe are end points, the boundaries of an argument in which I lose.

In the medieval clearing the suppers are now gnawing on bones and sucking at the lees from their cauldrons—a mile behind them, those old fucks, who back me less and less. They now, more clearly than ever, know that a poet is not to be trusted for a grant in an area outside of nonsense. Certainly not in anthropology—or archeology! What could a poet possibly know about stone! Or man! This is demonic. This is my testicle, the wild orchid in the lapel of pleistocene man! And Milton, badly wounded, does find van Gogh, in slum darkness several yards away from the pool table. Van Gogh is sawing through the radius of his dimension in order to crank sufficient purple, orange and fuchia into the bald light of the sauternes flavored night. Milton is all for hugging the table. The balls, the sticks, the sidewalk, the angels.

A homunculus named Om Ire stands up in my stomach. 41 years for him to compose on the threshold of my pelvis, under my heart which hangs over his left ear, grapes, he plucks, not "heartstrings," but ducks, clocks, tacks, oaks, he word tastes me, and Ira floats off, urine carried, no longer on his leaf bed bending one foot into his mouth, om body, uroboric. The leaf is his bier and his birth bed. Om Ire looks through me. When I make love he will see why he stands and why it has taken so long.

Have I accepted the smell of my insides? Is that the task of 41?

This homunculus is foundling. The sun. She loves him. Loves him? She lives him. Eats him. Why she? There are priests at his elbow, trying to drag him back to the awful ceremonies they insist keep the world running. Your world, you mean—he thinks—but already he has learned not to say. Why? He fears for his life? But how could that be, if where he is has no beginning? Could it have only an end? He looks at the blood running down his robe, his world, is that it running? "I keep remembering this story," he says to the priest, "it has no beginning or middle, only a funny end and then a disappear, as if the end were a segment of a story that went on . . . ."

"That was your message," one of them says, "do you want to

say it again?" "*Without death there would be no birth*," he says, hopeless, a homunculus . . .

IV

Carried on the arms of those old fucks, leech-ridden with failure to achieve their own sexuality. On the arms of those old fucks we attend funereal honor. To my father's funeral I go, on my own arm of old fuck. The oldest fuck. The not-fuck.

Of my course on the arm of not-fuck. Before the forest. In the shadow of king Oedipus. This would really sell if I could just titilate your cold, reader, if I could just keep you to freeze—which I cannot—fool you to think art meant to keep freezing in a new elegance, to relax in your extreme discomfort and find that you were relaxed.

Each spore must be watered again and again until another junior appears. Sex, as such, is table-setting. As a medieval middle-aged person, my desire is to blast those old fucks out of the rear of the suppers. Leave them, for a moment, without their shit.

Bitterness, inevitable. Even if one has not been cuckolded. The poem starts anywhere, agreed? Of course, anyone can agree on The Poem Starts Anywhere. Promiscuous. The poem, is promiscuous. Everyone agrees. I shake hands with those I detest. We agree. I am given a sheet of leper-shank—another is given a degree. We agree. Writing should be taught. Teach people how to read. But to recognize a leper? No one. Nor to recognize a poem.

A posthumous pardon for Sacco and Vanzetti. Those old fucks at work again! It is almost in cooperation with them that a medieval forest is erected, a tale of suppers, an image of a bleeding terrified chased woman. The same tale looked at for a moment is skeleton. An old man by a cactus watching two hungry creatures share a lizard. All things. As if all thought. All thinks. Ali crowds in. Ale hangs out at the edge of thinking. A kilogram. Someone, some way, to keep the mind alert in its fracture, lactifluous. Listen to what was said in that fragment. Of no wool in their cells. Of no worth in themselves.

149

Wolfless hells. A, a helpse. A shelter for errant elves. Can't you hear? I is a verb. A huge tome. Opium. A worb.

V

Where space is not in the dram, a dream tries to tssk aprons. Silly spot. How can I progress, I who believe in what I know and what I donut into the meadow, 12 years old. Why do those old fucks so bother you? They starve you into an early death? They feed you alcohol? So you adopt them, adapt. Those old fucks are the hollow layers of the first times you cannot remember. Do not be led into their aims. You know the cigar they lean on, the Havana Baptista Miami wink of Eldorado that does not slide or glisten. So Freud was wrong! To mismean is not to mean; to mismean is to honor a meaning glimpsed but unmeant. A slug in the sink does not articulate the blocked watcher. Always Robert Lowell around the corner, with a framed whaleboat, a living man composed of thousands of tiny safes! And to see him begging from frameless Jack Spicer! Spicer with his mirror seeking a frame from mirrorless Robert Lowell! One man on the toy train track of his birth, and the other? There is the track that stammers off, collecting the intestinal leaves that float down from the moon, and another, where lunar intestines have been precluded from the start.

This brings me to a family reunion. Lowell as well as Spicer. Olson as well as Gloucester. An ice-cream reunion, somehow between the stagnating suppers and those aging old fucks. Where a we takes place. Orphan weewee. The do bang on the tit cymbal.

Spicer's vision: is it to be pompromized by the intercrossing of unnamable demons from outer lace? Or are we only really galactizing on armor? Neither skin nor bluebeaten sky contacted? Getting off on the stars yet actually still ice-skating in the grooves of juvenalia? The shuck, the dead foliage, the splice in poetry, its fire-hydrant, that impacted place against experience, against the threshold of poetry, the moment of desire!

The poet hides someplace between religion and his pitiful personal lie. Ha! Not I, but the ghost stuffed through me! On one side

150

the forest, on the other those old fucks. The leathery ones, our own, those oldest fucks, the release prisms in our dream, slick brunettes, handsome encouraging fellows, Semensville, crossings, without crucifixion, that I be horizontal to you, unknown angel and you to me, vertical, chicken I just picked up in the cooler, can we, outside that old fuck, feel something for each other?

Hard, hard to feel anything outside that old fuck, since he claims in my mind to be before me, a gold chained cock that leads down and down into bright blue vater, eh fater? Down into bedouin, down into Arabic vise, where women are squeezed dye, so they only exhibit a color on our shoulders, us cool ones, with our indigo misery like veins sewn across our olders, we fear, we white ones, seeking stone lesion we fear that if we do find "it" the rain will not spawn awning?

Be well, old fuck, and keep your seminar coffin, be elf, mold muck, suck and do not eke out the meaning before your censor; fame? Oppose it with all your clay. Her meaning? Incognito at the end of a tomb as a vine pushes through. Pushy, life says. Her meaning. As if it could plait milk.

Her meaning. Man has remained so narrow, a church, a duplicate pillar, less, a trickle, shackled by the extent to which male ice cubes have controled the growth of asters. As if Harlem were to be computed Washington. Or Iran, Liberace. Or horizontal slaves under deck planks to erupt back the boot slime they swallowed.

I am going to recontact Satan, to open the teeth of his flame and to inspect his gums. Under my adversary are two poets in satanasis.

JOSEPH

I am very concerned about you—especially
since yesterday, when I realized just how long
you have been dressed like Blondie,
imprisoned in the frame in which she sits
on a stool, trying on hat after hat . . .

Yesterday, a terrible command fell
like a long drip out of a dream, as if I had heard
it upon waking, differently, but as the day sloughed its color,
this monster struck: "Why have you not returned Hitler's tits?"

I thought of your son, the European Jesus,
the Grünewald strength with which he still
gangrenes, in amber light, as if infested with an enormous botfly,
about to burst, in the mind of the cathedral
which thus rushes in sunlight, everywhichway,
which of course never reaches him, but radiates in place,
high, where the energy of the emasculated young
forever remains, in "heaven"—

when I was asked why I had not returned
Hitler's tits I saw you, Joseph, trying on various crowns of thorns,
a kind of Blondie, as if "Hitler's tits" were the latest fashion,
as if the pain of what people do to people, jumbled up
in my unconscious, had appeared, in drag, trying on
various head frames which had been decorated with "Hitler's tits."

The crown of thorns, on one hand, a cliché, and, on the other, the
consort of whatever force it has met in my unconscious, something so
irrational it seems as if I were joking. But female tits on the devil

152

reveal him to be in the service of generation—he is not satanas, the adversary, after all, not the ancient poet dressed up in skins who I still believe I argue with when I argue, so that when one says "the devil is loosed in the world" possibly one means that the adversary has been released from the tension binding him to his equal, the bond has snapped, and the two ends whip about wildly, frightened people clump together and ponder the father and the son,

but the angel/devil differentiation tells us that the moment of desire has been purified and debased, the see-saw of eye to eye relationship has turned into generation, the generations, experience versus innocence, and the poet exists to be the adversary's equal—his active engagement is the satanas, or the other, the defying particular person whose creative thought runs against the former's grain. But the poet is at the same time riding the waves of the passivity of people which would like to incorporate his energy in the way that people draw energy from food.

Somehow, Joseph, you appeared in these thoughts, as the poet who did not fight to keep the child an equal argument between people, but who allowed the child to become on one hand, mystical flesh, and, on the other, fleshy spirit—so that the argument belongs to no one, the sexual process is denied and consequently imagination is forced to live on a house of stilts, since the joy of sexual encounter, which grounds and seeds imaginative activity, has been pulled away, leaving just fantasy, terrible fantasy figures stripped of meaning, Hope, Crosby and Lamour, the mind punning off itself, the cheapest clichés, sexual meaning bottled up in jokes, taxes, adultery, the world of fringe . . .

you, Joseph, you are the twist, or starch in the waterfall, the fraying agent, where the connection between two is vacated. In my desire to fix contours to what I am saying, I overload you. Historically, you have suffered enough, yet something about you keeps me obsessively digging here; you gave up your fatherhood to the amalgamation of your childhood fear of your father—or your awe of your father—you were willing to agree that your time in Mary did not happen—something like your dream of your father when you were a little boy, that huge omnipotent otherness, he was in Mary all

153

along, so when you penetrated her, wasn't it as if you had strapped his coffin about your loins, a dildo construction built out of your fear of life? Yet she was pregnant—your wood ancestral cock which carried your misuse of your own and her life—this, your father and his father, all those hyenas, were grouped about the kill, your living cock, the father hyena and the grandfather hyena, hungry, to have some of the kill, and as you stared at it, she was responsible, she was bringing life, your child, to die and to face you dying.

Was she, before, in your dreamtime, your satanas? The power of the argument, as an equal give and take, eye to eye, was gone, but was that the dream you gave up on? That Jesus, the holy child, was the failure to come to conclusion between living child and imaginative child, a physical child was to be born, so the two of you would have that experience, and then your own soul was to become worth something that you alone, by her, could know, could not inherit, could not see, as flesh, before you, but could only realize in otherness, like stone or trapped and skinned sound,

your meaning, what you had not been given, yet was present along the edges of your eyes when they looked straight and vulnerable into the eyes of who you loved . . .

but Joseph, I have to make most of this up, and when it seems clear, it is only for a moment, I say satanas to satanas, as if that healthy contention would ray out, touch, and inform . . .

the size of the log you rested on while it burned is enormous now, invisible, mechanical, and increasingly generational—millions of children come up to you where you drowse, in flames, your arm about Mary, blackened, smoldering, they want to know how you can stand to relax and dream about God . . .

154

VARIATIONS DONE FOR JOHN DIGBY

The jig is sawed. Puzzle
up. What is missing
parts, the 19th century
lass, buckled in fur,
boots, plumed hat,
is missing Baron
Lion who approacheth
wrapped in Biblical curtains,
the weight of that century!
Lizards, sparrows, skunks
begin to emerge from the under-
clothing, what shaman
cartoons the Victorians were!
Bound in the plumage of
the earth, they swam to bed,
footlights below them glowed,
Baron War approacheth,
deluge laps the lamp-posts.
In bird mind there was instruction to
Max Ernst, for each bird discovered
its lower body increasingly
trousered, its nest inhabited
by human-headed worms putting on
clothing over clothing
to build a Babel of clothing, to
reach orgasm? Or was that Heaven
glinting through the dragon folds?
Air-tight puzzle, the missing
part more and more swollen,
August, and the men of Cambridge

are punting through the rye,
their collars strong as crash-helmets,
through the filigree of their lasses
they snuck in African booty,
picnic in the swamp, the missing
part, an ape they thought, was
entertained at night, gas-light night,
the pulp of bird song was papered into
wall pattern, a hunting scene
still haunts English poetry:
the hound halts a moment before it is
seized by the fox's death, strikes
a pose, raising its tail
angular feminine buttocks are
set between gore and the hunter's
desire, the fox flesh served
by wenches is gulped
through a muzzle, the poet's tongue
touches his gale through a screen,
through candle flame Vincent's
hand, half burned, nuzzles the incestuous
coils of Gaugin's eyes,
all these visions lay a dry veil
over dreaming Cambridge,
Caryl and I visted in spring 1974,
the icy walks swirled without
recourse into Blake's gold leaf—
from his Marriage I looked back to
Yeats outside the Fitzwilliam,
Blake's loaf of excrement had been turned
into bread, the world was eatable,
me too, a caterpillar, and as I
passed through myself
a pair of blood spats remained.
Our faces are more and more like hours,
our hours are more and more rectangular
sores set stained glass, a veined

and circular story; a winged Victorian
fairy is way below on his knees,
a muscular Victorian fairy
with abalone dragonfly wings,
he is praying against the hardened
pelt of each present moment for the punters to
worm down their poles, for the oak
to cease to be an inverted
buried man—what I lean into
is perhaps the crotch of a critic,
it feels and looks like oak
but the vibration is damaged rainbow,
so damaged the creatures can hardly
cross its bridge; Noah keeps beckoning
from the childhood pillow afloat
in what the threshing-machine gives—
I offer up my semen as all
colors flee the rainbow but red,
scarlet, cream and maroon,
                                        poetry
is a chill glass of wine half buried in Death Valley.

IN THE POLLUTED CORNICE OF THE DAY

a pearl of wheat forms,
a Jackson Pollock mandala,
shoulder dip wrist lash.
The stone legs of giant gate guardians
are leaned against him while he paints.

*

His alcohol is on his head.
Under his feet inspissant silence.
To his right a bull, draped "female symbol,"
to his left a horse, draped "male symbol,"
are sadly watching him web.

*

The jelly of movement encased,
a clock circles within bone.
I'm ticked off, a fuse leading its fusion by
the spark. As I get older
the sides of life become denser dreams.

*

In the guardian's leg is the shrine
I had thought he was guarding behind him:
Louis C. Tiffany, crosslegged on velvet,
shows me red glass streaked with brighter reds,
inverted fire balloons with large necks.

158

*

A dragonfly sips the jasmine in his veins.
The incense is so veiling I begin to think Beauty
is the metachrosis of organs
into pseudo-natural forms, "nothing ugly,"
Tiffany always insisted, "art must be beautiful."

*

Outside, in the medieval Japanese wind,
Pollock has been strung up.
I watch the way air interlocks with life's
fluted edges, sinew to
an opalescent idiot toying with a bat.

*

Over the radio just now news that Tiffany
is considering adopting Jackson.
Under the radio the spider hands out its news:
it is Pollock's stomach in which Louis C. sits,
restored of course to its former Moroccan design.

*

I'm still pulled to believe in a "whole picture,"
as if the triangle were the square's "better half."
That pull, although I have torn out my roots,
is the straining infant hand, the Bodhi tree shade
always not always titilating beyond it.

*

Between the guardian legs, Pollock is whirls
in which minerals corruscate
devotional forms. Telodendritic kinesis.

By each flung tendril the end is daily
lanced, branching the boil of his duco misery.

OM HOLLOW

Around person,
the ghost of house,
chalk lines, aura,
so crisscrossed
he seems composed of dabs,
weavings, strata,
a jerking halt process,
unending, the end is
set deep, as if
Newton's fruit
could be returned to the limb.

*

Something moves.
A lobster? In the murk,
lobes stirring?
A web of lodes?
What is really here?
One thing is sure:
whatever is is housed.
Carapace. Frost poncho.
Headless, the archai
drift down the mountain.
Moving around my head
while writing is done.
Is this theirs? Whose ours?

*

"My house is not my house," Lorca gasped
as Goya's *Cinco de Mayo* riflemen fired.
At five in the morning,
wolf hour, when the Seine ice
spidercracks, a dead poet's face
is mine, all of this is
all of their
gar bled tongues,
even the cornice, the vermicelli
in the cello shaped cellar.
There is music below.
For it the archai descend,
they want to drink music.

*

If I reach out quickly
I snatch traces. 4705 is only
the nearest dust of the chalk
outline, the cool
my hand brushes only the swell
of my 188 pound Indiana tear.
Put my hand in further
and the shoulder of one turns,
under its frost poncho,
away—it thinks I want to flay it,
to wear its hollow.

*

The archai followed Orpheus wanting drink.
Killer bees moving up from Brazil,
archai returning to their peaks.
What is not
the ones we are
composed of?
Our work is to become immortal.
To gnash here to assert the flame free.

                *

"You are
immortal," the archai
whispered through Jack Spicer.
Said this while they played on him.
Children on a jungle gym.
Vermicelli. Then fled having
drunk drunk Jack.
The plink of icicle water
forming in his glass.

                *

Our work is to imagine what we are.
Artaud's way was to build an anal door, a poetry
to vie with the poetry of the rose.
A house of skin with Xipe obsidian.
A door up into the Muladhara Chakra
from where he could see the male
hollow under his heart,
the cemetery breeding grounds of the human
"tree."

*

Where I can't conceive
or carry a child
is Om Hollow.
Trying to fill in.
Fainting against the prayer wall.
Weeping and pounding against
the wall around Om Hollow.

*

The "eternity" shaped silence inside.
The sound of an ice
sickle cutting ice
men. Even the archai go
down. On each other, lobsters.
Devouring music.
I envision them in Om Hollow
sporting with the women men call "girls."

*

The inside outline begins to emerge:
the baby misery
of having been nursed by a mother alone.

*

Father, scattered in a Set of shadows, Osiris-
wound hand passings against brown (my first color
6 days old I remember
over my crib

      *

The icicle he placed, instead, in my mouth.
A dripping, a
cave depression, he placed
bare distance in my mouth, I
ogled, beaking so
wide her nipple became
needle.

      *

With perforated
brow, looking
back and forth between mother
and linoleum,
make sense of this, she said, wallpapering
the bars of my crib,
make sense of what I,
pillow, and bar,
have dressed you in,
nowhere with you at center.
Every
where
was a bottle around which
I felt my own thigh, I tried to pick up a rubberband,
it was nailed

with her fall.
She cuts the cold
to the size of my blanket.
That is her unending embrace.

      *

At the base of the Om Hollow wall,
phantom packed men.
Our ears against it.
Inside is it windy or calm?
Glacial
or eden?
Men, agrimechanic weevils.
Building swear mansions out of our wonder.

DANSE MACABRE

The verse of Crane John Chamberlined,
crane chamber where shakoed English elves
salute the collapse of a 6 century long tongue
rolled out turf of opalescent clams.
Could there be more fin rot
Pierre, off England, than in Biscayne Bay?
Crowbarred genes, a peach neon gleam in the pink
cauliflowers on white suckers' lips,
haute cuisine hues in oil slick drugstores,
porgies in Victorian ruffles bent
over pickax stew, susurrant surreal catasta
in the side of the bluegill, not merely its bones but
Theseus grappling with the Minotaur,
enter the double ax and immediately swerve right
then left to depart, but what are the two natures
that clash once the center is found?
The nature that is meander versus the nature that is centered,
transgression versus obedience,
solar orientation to the father pole
versus the animal lines looping and crossing, cut
into the intestinal walls of Les Combarelles,
I make out a salmon in stone a bison intersects
swerves that are still fresh gash, the sap
of the rock still luminescent, I imagine a mind
which did not see a tree as outreach of trunk
but, in its tumble walk on earth, as a corseted
mass of roots writhing at both ends—
now barbwire around Stonehenge, the monolith and her court
so corralled they begin to buck in imagination
a threshing-floor where Ariadne is clawing the hero's mind alive,

is she the offspring of the 14 foot cave bear
lurking in the maze of paleolithic night?
Like meeting Carcharodon—did they dance against Carcharodon?
The shark of the land and the swimming bear, early constellations,
certain catfish now snap their backbones while swimming,
Walter Kandrashoff observed black mullets   [*New Times,*
with tumors dangling off their body like grapes,   May 13, 1977]
performance on a susurreal catasta where the woman is
sawed in half, then the magician runs off,
his name is Bruckner, he has been ordered to
return to his organ, "a clam playing an accordion"
may be the image a clam's agony tremor now makes,
poetry twitches with this snapping in process,
snappers with tumors about their mouths from feeding at
sewage outlets, something suffers in me because
I don't fight pollution literally every day,
this is the Rabelais kick back, the feast now looks like Japanese
plastic display food except it is polychlorinated biphenyls
mixing with ocean, I might as well be 11 year old Rimbaud
pouring over an octopus, the two hand in tentacle
up childhood's road, sentimental cigar-box picture
trudging into the sunset, that same octopus
exploding in the buttocks of Bellmer wraiths,
to hold in mind the fresh paleolithic salmon and
the fin rotted pin fish fills me with elastic venom,
I still see the elevator in Charlie Myers Department Store
on Washington off Meridian, Eichmann is riding in a crystal
Aztec skull from floor to floor, from strata to strata,
through the middens, my father insisted
on keeping his hat on regardless of what happened
in the floor lamp department of that path
in My Lai Soutine saw turn into a raw bentipede,
the earth shakes loose wounds to show its pompano
surface,
          the postman rings, my monthly Donald Duck,
wrapped in a menstrual fishrag, interrupts my Danse Macabre.

LES COMBARELLES

Shape in
the cyclone at
ox-rib. A scratch.
A core meandering.
Acorn, forced.
Let me open is still our cry
as if we are behind the sun.
I'm not bitter. It is just that I am still at
ox-rib. A nut-like flavor
where I think I should yield
mass. Or glory. Starting
41 years ago
15,000 years too late.
With the anger of 3 zeros,
with historical need
to see myself backwards, as if I
were a line
vegetal-certain
which ended with a root.
As if my shape
grasped my condition
instead of merely responding
as if there were a center
yoked to
the material around it,
cutting into, thus with walls,
securities, deposits,
a quarry out of which
my figure is specific, meander,
but with a core, as if I could not

merely travel
a line in stone, a tiger forehead
finding its way through Les Combarelles
is linked to stallion, a stalled
lion, the forehead line is crossed
by bearclaw, a hut
is made, nothing in mind goes on and on,
leaves
lay Persian on colorless ground,
passionately I appeared with Caryl to
step toward the cave mouth under trees
shit themselves
upward, then relaxed
leaves and lost
the man they stamped me with, father,
if transformations go on and on
there would be no point
where a center could be fixed,
there would be a grail
partially visible in the Bel-Aire Hotel pond
and I would get my blood's worth every
inhalation, there is a grail
in the whooping-cough tent and a grail
tied about the swan's neck, I
let the grail foam over,
step on leaves with Caryl, inside 15,000 years,
getting to the hole, in which I see arms,
like a ring about a coffee cup, linked,
love, the word, is so burned out it starts
to come back again, a scalded child,
spirit, starts to come back again,
core, me/and/her, starts to come back again,
kachkaniraqmi, starts to define again,
"in spite of everything we still are,
we still exist with all the possibilities for
reintegration and growth."

THE RANCID MOONLIGHT HOTEL

All books are "dirty"—
they are built out of stimulated organs.
"And what about love?" the Cal Arts student,
a woman, asked Carlos Castaneda.
"Oh you mean fucky fucky fucky?" Carlos squealed,
bumping and grinding for the whore
in army overcoat and combat boots
outside the SAC Compound in Seoul,
I went with her because I wanted to see
the unpainted board of the repression of desire;
her hotel was built of rancid moonlight,
her swarthy caked body pawed about
filching the bills from my crumpled
bedsprings, for you see I was not there
but strung out along those alleys listening
to the plank heart of Indiana, a skyscraper
outhouse, or is it a lighthouse,
in place of a beam a lit diorama
where an aligator, dressed in a diaper,
is being bound up in branches, kindling
for the 20th century auto-da-fé.
Isn't it time you stopped roasting Indiana?
You can't burn out a state of mind
that you will never fully understand,
thus your fight, like all others,
merely turns the vise
tighter against that crash course, culture,
since most humanistic effort
has been to pin the diaper on the aligator,
to toilet train a tree so it phallocratically

becomes "human," yet Albion slumps to his rock
having just fallen asleep during
an embrace in The Rancid Moonlight Hotel,
of course he "fell" so he doesn't have to watch
the ugly clay model he made of his desire
playing with his rubber aligator
in his Egyptian steam-bath sandbox—
as if her back could be unzipped
and a lovely strong woman prowl away—
what I expected to unearth in that Hotel,
the continental divide, or, the banister
children slide squealing, unhurt, before the shadow
of Carlos Castaneda bumping and grinding
on the Mexican desert while some old
Indian sot, his audience, thumps the ground with
that whore's body, for
the fact is, she won't come apart,
no cougar lady leaves her,
nor is there a model
husk lying on the sand.
What endures is her hunger
which she herself will not face
dragging a confused American up those rancid steps,
the wound tight toy of childhood
is not released, but sat on, or
surrounded by her fist and crushed just enough
for him to look back through the Christmas tree years
to glimpse a web entangled with cauls, various instruments,
like knees, Incan lobotomies, the aligator,
without diaper, dressed in his brain.

DIALOGUE WITH A TRIPTYCH

When I asked why the house appeared intact,
complete, yet also collapsing away, its rugged
ruddy shadows ready to be packed in the smallest valise—
he answered, "You see, the key is in
drawing the door open as I enter the door
to depart, flashing only a bulbous profile, this white
door I draw my body into, barberpoling my left leg—
it is not so much a description of leaving
as a construction of what has been left,
namely the world screens, canvases,
my dimension, more shadow now
than anatomy, slides into what I draw, and my arms,
well, you see what I have done with them . . . "
They are the hardest part to make sense of,
I said, their muscles have been sprung, they are knotty
yet flacid, and bear no connection to your suit.
"Think of them as clock hands which are now
pinned on the door itself and only by accident
does the right reach up and draw, and the left
in some obscure octopus motion reach consolingly
for my left shoulder; they are whiter than flesh
because of my blind-drawn, lobby nature, and the right
is set against a fresh blood shadow, a limb
floating on the surface of a depthless pool
I guess, to insist that my arm be seen even though
its white is the same as the door that draws me . . . "
That draws *you*, I queried—"Yes," Bacon continued,
"that draws me in to the left and right panels of the work,

where a lavender paler than white backdrops two
isolate figures perched on the edge of two circus
rings, what has been left is Dyer's headstone to
the right and the self-grappling man, whose shadow
now begins to resemble a diaphanous pallet,
to the left—you see Dyer swerving, in silence of course,
his head away from my opening the door; his headstone
sets firmly on one ring's edge and his profile and bust
fall directly forward to be caught through a cocktail table
which, since there is only background below it, appears
to be hinged to the ring and his headstone; I have done the table
sky blue to allow the reflection of his head to continue
to fall through the table's edge—a minor matter,
perhaps, but since I have set his stone into the work,
sky becomes precious, a kind of jewel blue I allow to
surface in that place we leaned on, discussed, spilled drinks . . . "
And the other figure, I reminded him, the one you called
"the self-grappling man." "Well, he revolves around me
as a second wheel, or cog, and where his teeth meet
with those of Dyer's, I interlock—I mean, the self-
grappling man swings into the dead beloved, who grappled
with me, and that, in a sense, is where my world
watersheds, between the man knotted into his own
ball of twine, and the man whose cock and hands are
ceaselessly intertwined with another man's. These two
of the work float free now that Dyer is gone—
though you will notice that behind the self-grappling one
a shadow of possibly two rather faints into the pale
lavender; such is his ghost, as is the ghost of
Dyer Narcissus, as the headstone image falls
through the urn grip of its sky blue table pond . . . "

While he was speaking, I noticed he kept his head turned
to the left, away from Dyer, though his body
doored, appeared to veer in the direction of Dyer's
rotating ring, "I am aware of that," he almost
whispered, "in a way something about me wanted to

hold open the door I was drawing and let the one sail
into the other, wanted to remain a third, neither self-
grappling nor in contact with another." Can you
tell me something about this third, I pressed.
"It is a phase of life, a stage one begins to glimpse
when one realizes one is alone, and in that sense,
self-grappling—one sees it dimly, *through* something,
as it were, and that something becomes the other
as one matures or, even if one never matures,
out of loneliness seizes some other to adore and touch,
and in doing so, the third is heart-breaking, for
in contact with the other it seems split between what
grapples with itself and the very nature of the third:
to be grappled with by one's materials so that the door
opens one as one draws the door, so that one stands
doored when one stands at all, on hinges, of the nature of
the door one is drawing open, which is closed of course
on one. It is rather like being alive outside the death
that is quickly erasing the contours of what one thought
one had lived—thus the whole tent show lightens,
and as one's entire house buckles, as its crimson is
invaded by lavender's neutral truth, the two rings over
which elephants stepped when one was a boy
slowly rotate, bearing, as if on an airport carousel,
heart luggage, anonymous, their contents fully known."

[This triptych, called "Triptych
1971," is reproduced as #5 in
the catalog prepared by Galerie
Claude Bernard, in Paris, for
Francis Bacon's show of recent
work there in 1977. Bacon himself
has insisted that it be specified
that this poem is based on an
imaginary interview.]

CANSO

This July, how pleased I am, and bereaved,
how multitudinous the flares, the ires and air that
match me, that ignite and
extinguish the shifting hearth
I hold to, alone from you,

a gentle rabbit through whom lightning passed,
how I love you through, and how
as you heal, I study the model you gave me,
when we met, decent beauty
where the pearl is in the oyster lips,

not separable, you are sore
but you walk, more upright each day,
and I rejoice, making use of the spirit of
Marcabru, Vidal, those 12th century sweethearts,
those throat stones of our vers, homage to those

one-tracked singers, who drove admiration and
obsession for love through, our first caterpillars,
the first eaters whose leaves we have council,
soon Blackburn's complete *Proensa* will appear,
leaf, translation and my Caryl,

bundled in July, a bouquet, how glad to adorn
her room and spirit, mist and shaper of
this home, how strange to think of her
in canso, how marvelous, to hear
the strains of adoration intact, so near

in distance, my love for her will never
debrim its well, at least as long as I rage or
range, is it, and give? And take from the garden,
the eternity, which is our portion, and not
some uncomposed other, I have been blessed

finding myself in alignment with her measure.
Which is heaven, sure, here, the uncoupled garden
wherein Eve and Adam recoup the serpent pliancy
before the fang, an ancient hardness, acted in
our minds to reject the gratitude of

someone with his or her beloved. How I yearn for you,
having not embraced you during your convalescence.
And how delicious it is to sit by the fidelity stone,
and feel polished, awful, clear, without reward,
and know that stone, in haircloth,

while surrounded by such corpulent timber.
Those troubadors, what ax spun below their grind?
Was this the pleistocene condition,
to feel the lark of axcension, as
the slipknot of the word curled and stroked itself?

No, I am not angry at the doctor, his pulling
you open, I have to heal, and burn off about you,
not sick myself. Homage to those who yearned
before, who, were they here, would try
to drink me under once they saw and heard

your voice, which I hear, as you offer me, your thought,
about our workings, something obscure passes and then you,
asleep now, healing, become such gold again—
has Paul visited me tonight? Welcome, Paul,
if you are here, your voice in these lines,

vidas and razos is the parent-power, I happily share,

oak-sense, burrow-meat, my god Paul
are you here? Not as Sorrentino's remembered drunk
but as clos, clime, cilicious cleaver, ah
you fade, you do not want anyone to be put down.

Caryl, you are home, how delicate
is the tilt of hearth, you are not muse or lady
yet I adore you in this sense
because I am turning the troubador condition
backward and forward, like bending a clock handwise,

and handwise distilling the metal self,
spreading the hands all over the face of
the terms that occur in poetry, this oldest
historical shape—recognition and desire—
peals my gladness to be with you, again.

A LATE EVENING IN JULY

for John and Barbara Martin

A certain amber, a gate light, a tawny orange, fresh
in mist, under palms, and the darkened white
stucco under Spanish tile—
                              one imagines stained
glass in the side of such a house,
inside, a piano and bookcases,
the night is such deep indigo mist.

Yet one never sees inside—
inside is the mind's dream of Friday, of a mutuality
where no one sleeps, or if sleepers be,
they are dreaming spinnets, pages muffled
in Russian snow, and if there is blood,
it will be digested, as conscience,
in a dreaming reader's mind . . .

The amber gate light is more and more beacon to one more
and more off and on shore, because the tree
shapes are less dark, though dark they are,
than the amber edge evoking hearth, and more,
the grave illusion of what happened, which will
never happen, but which is, gold
splinters indigo misericordia, enchased
in visible night, the steady starfish
hearse of Santa Barbara, as if this scent
could be taken, as one animal takes another,
digested and adored . . .

Yet it is nothing, again, is happening.
The soft chill, the Crusoe rustle are so special

because the contact is more than one could ever
be to oneself without such forms, without
such buried carnival. When one was less bulk,
younger, these vibrations passed
from pore to port, boats ahum
as if the ocean weight did not exist.

One ages, and the meanings in amber and white
repeat, nourish, even though one is reined to
that Crusoe ghost, one's mind, that
light, stucco, mist ignore.

A warmth that these washed isles are brothers
announces the basil yearnings of maturity
for the sunflecks of a maternity now disclosed,
yet forever mysterious. The amber, the stucco
white, at noon not even fixed upon,
are latent and raised, Lazarus, in all things,
even the arch unruffled shades
one knows but cannot substantiate are trees.
Are one sitting here. As the gentle waves,
nothing's chrestomathy, layer summer with
the unsowed lax salt of autumnal seed.

STUDY OF A MAN STARING AT A PILLOW IN THE DARK

She is there and not there, always to live
even when dead, because he was and is
her child. Should he tell her she is dying?
Because she prefers to spare him news,
should he say nothing about this so she will
not suffer thinking of him knowing?
But if she already knows, then his saying nothing
will establish nothing as a kind of glass
between them, he will visit her
as one visits a prisoner, with whom one talks
through a partition watched. Yet to tell her nothing
becomes the possibility of saying it clearly,
of sharing his dead fact, which will always dream
of her alive, with her in such a way that she
hears we in his broken Doric,
for surely her condition has cracked his I;
he appears intact, but that column
which until now has resisted spinal waves of we
which would carry I under, is broken in place,
and as he raises himself up on one elbow to stare
at what is doubling and subtracting each hour,
this face watching him from his Siamese pillow,
this semi-mirror, always less him, thus
more and more her, this pillow is the platter
no one is severed upon, and no one is him,
severed to his mother's side. He must say
nothing and say it so it lives, or remain
self-purgatoried in a cunt-hexed mirror.
Unsaid, nothing has a death of its own, a shape

men have made from not sharing nothing
with their dying mothers. They robe what is unsaid,
they insert a skeletal hag under its Hindu silk,
knives and mugs of blood on her wheel of arms,
they take what has broken inside and,
in one simultaneous gesture, place themselves, gangrenous,
below and in Kali, place themselves, heroic,
above and through any woman whom they crucify
Scarlet.   .

LIFE THEN SEEMS THICKER

Only after Caryl came home and was recovering
did that "then" begin. She was fresh, yet
her suffering in Cedars-Sinai now seemed to
go on behind the fruit, as if Zurbarán occluded
the meaning of the fruit's source of light,
as if that black hung between the fruit   [Still-life, with
and Zurbarán's Caryl, let me imagine   Lemons, Oranges
his wife was ill and that her cot   and a Rose]
was placed in a cold fall orchard
attended by nuns who would drink of
their own pitchers, lift up their habits and wring them
into their own mouths when Caryl Zurbarán called.
At $160 a day. Translated into their nourishment, not hers.
And as I passed the wall, on the way to my Caryl,
did Caryl Zurbarán's cry tar that black, did it
heat that flat, was my Caryl in black, her abdomen cut,
the white I felt, her face, out of spectrum,
did a sort of still-life within
a still-life take her spectre and run it through my white,
so that those hoof-sized lemons were a spaceless altar,
a moment, passing, twice a day,
and now, to feel them

one dimensional, but meaning more.

My spectre, which will not accept Zurbarán,
wants to tear away his black background
and see a scene, there is something about art
that is always an infuriating plain.
Here, black sand swirls off into a layered ark,

183

the tumult Caryl's operation engendered
still raises waves which I milk to spar tips,
it is as if Atlantis were a bob, a cater,
yet the matter of emotion now speeds out flat,
flattening the primal, leaving the air, the dream air, flat.

Then/thin, an I, our ego, is difference.
On any desert near people an altar can be found.
I, a doric pillar,
                             a rugose
scarlet fever to be beyond the self, iced,
sitting?
                   Where the archai are not, are teli.
Caravaggio is caracoling in the background

of Zurbarán's englished lemons,

                                         the file that stood within
each joist of house, use, nothing is clear in reproduction,

                                                        I turned
from the elevator outlet,

Zurbarán, you are magnificent absence, your still-life

sets its fruit, grand mother father grace
before me, fruit of light lit by Caravaggio's headless neck.
The knife of background fruitsets. How

walk the halls of Cedar-Sinai is dinosauric umbo.
How feel her tray is the rose

a cry bulbed with rooted blue.

THIS I CALL HOLDING YOU

In contrast to you,
I sometimes think
horror pornography,

a woman alone
on her back tumbling
with her feet
the empty
barrel of no one.

Our love-making
swift bullseye
ripples out,
throws a lavender
through the police-flasher sun,
entering you
I'm concentrated in a breaker.

The opaque in life
is not seen through,
those who claim to see through it
are seen through
opaquing the felt

density of experience,
the surface carcan
traffic at noon, or having to wash
dishes when I want to pump
bullets through Idi Amin
made out of his victims.

Over you, in you,
what it means is perhaps more
than it does, you penetrate me
and my over you puts me on all fours
(to murder him with the flesh of his victims)
the raw plank

of what you mean,
a splinter-cushion,
the cock is so manifold,
a man, I fold, within the mind of my cock,
the voodoo needles of
cannot see through,
                    you penetrate me,
your sides penetrate my hands,
this I call holding you—

flat, quickly fabricated contemporary day
against the thickness of Bruckner's 7th,
its density to assimilate the
fragrance of your breasts and my desire
as I am stroked, deep in you, to touch
their soft, they are clouds
in which infants are sleeping,
                    bear Amin,
bear the Chicano burglars in skier masks who
forced the woman bartender to suck each of them off,
your breasts are clouds but not auraed
with deadly 18th century Boucher cherubs flitting
about the rape of Europa, up in the clouds
to divorce violence from its earth adherence.

All of me does want to enter you,
to know the thrust of the middle body to
bring in the whole person, not merely the man
to paint, as if in a woman, a cave's insides

but the woman to travel along the cock's edges
and squeeze between the sun and the moon
and aromatize the night sky!
                                    Tonight you stepped
out of the Datsun backseat, as off a shell,
writhing up out of the seat-belt tackle and I was aged
in image, a mage at sea, porous to my father's fum,
his padding sounded, fum fum, foam fum,
ah, your Aphrodite-flavored lace . . .

But I've been brewed in a patina
where "over you" reads out "control over you."

You step off these shells
in the sense that you step off my eyes
and the meaning of entering you
is a guide to behavior. Since your soft there
is moist and wants me

why do I fear the night?
Swift bullseye ripples out, alleluia
rowers reach the pond shore and pull
me out gaping, wanting to swallow the moon,
wrenched crosswise, a swastika on the pour of directions.

I stay up late to penetrate the carnal cape,
but I won't play hearts—
I know each scissorbill of my cock's vanity,
each noose of its trumped aces,
each image fainting before the chaos of
no new image to come, no image wanting
to naturally divide, each wanting to enmoat,
wall off and live forever, a crypt in which The Holy Family
scrubs The Three Bears, in which Sluggo,
humiliated by the cock as unthinkable dangle,
fondles the elderly queen of his adolescent flush,
erecting inside me as I become erect,

my infant feeling at that moment
that he is very warm, that his bowels
are acceptable as soup, that what is brown
floats in the sun itself—

he goes in with a wheelbarrow,
he comes out with a wheelbarrow filled.
Vaginal gossip. The Semen Daily.

I watch him pass into you with
his caul lantern, he is the vulnerable
little person who goes in ahead of me and returns
with the mystical impulse to indoctrinate and withdraw,
locking into and cogging others
less pitch pointed than oneself,
so that the cog angle of approach
is a Scientologist on a street corner
encysted with carcan need to turn, as a gear,
against the steel collarspike of another.

What is thought of as sex today
is a blister over earth,
the earth itself has swollen up
our misuse of it, people fumbling to spurt or leak
or leaking inside or spurting through a newspaper hole on the sub-
    way,
it is that deadness I hate, which my infant
with a mortar of hod instead of semen wearily carries back and forth.

SKEEZIX AGONISTES

Unwrap me, the witness said.
So I lifted his glass enclosure,
undid his Pope robes, his jockey shorts,
unscrewed his penis, collecting
the stale water in my little pail—
so here I stand, with this wormhusk in my arms,
a witness you, my hearer,
listen through. Is nothing

essential in what I see?
Take this tan stucco wall next door, its window
reveals a replay of Samson in Vietnam,
a living TV episode in the CIA
translation of its Pinochet into its penis Shah
—or do I have it backwards?
Is it the Shah's country-length organ
Donald and his nephews are displaying to the gestapo
debutants in Chile? Could I, as a cultural
attaché, observe the medieval
clockwork of these phallic translations?
(immediately the driveway between Washington and LA
fills with dodos, millions of 'em, motionless,
now I get the game: find the shell who's laid an egg . . .)

So, I'm in the grace of difference, where nothing,
smug enough to begin to define itself, is rolling and laughing,
a jellyfish, behind John Ashbery's ermine-lined boredom,
the nothing that leads a child to think Daffy is a duck,
that adjusts the visuality of the cartoonic landscape, no blur
but so much boinging information that any wall,

once reflected upon, is a stop sign billboard maze of signals,
and I dream of an iridic void, I dream of chopping
straight down, around the base of my room,
through the entire planet, to turn my base into a pillar
where saint-like I might sit, talking to myself in broken Doric . . .

but off the edge of my right palm
someone who I will never be is shouldering
the mill wheel for my Breakfast of Shampooed ions
—and nothing, are you merely the most recent fig leaf?
When I lift you, do I see Sweet Pea's
nearly extinguished infant face
or is that a chemical substitute, a wax
mouth organ, sugared, for chewing, not playing?

Nothing, you must be why I daily awake
with a baby dinosaur's face and fall toward the floor
turns, as I fall, because I am an American, it goes
swinging through space before me, we come round,
what was to be struck is being chased,
a rotation, the new firewheel
set out on an Iranian field
where schoolchildren are grazing their lunch—
at times they must look up and glimpse
my not-being-floored deflowered "No truth
for which I could die" spinning.

ALL WHITE HANDS ON DECK

Within the black students' voices,
the friction against speaking white
is drawing a mountain range on the blackboard.

I wonder, am I visible on their wavy line,
and if so, where? Below, as the mountains valley,
or on a peak, so far from the base
each neighboring peak floats unconnected . . .

Chances are, we are all between, discrete and contiguous,
free only in the friction we imagine, less white
than the voice prints between us, far less black
than the board on which the students face
instruction, chalked on, then dusted off,
which they are to absorb, as if they are mountains,
snowed daily, freezing over to evaporate
in sunlight to be snowed again . . .

Is to not snow them to leave them with their color?
I'd like to bring out the mountain in their color
and, to draw the color from their mountain,
for they *are* mountains! With long vine-like legs and arms
which lie entangled on the classroom floor
while the mountains sit and stare.
Unable to reach their peaks
I go off into their valleys, I watch an African child
suddenly weaned to make way for his baby sister
bloat with protein deficiency, kwashiorkor,
wean of hunger, I place you in this line,
I understand my participation, as an American,

in the cannibalization of that child,
but this is no more than offering my word
to an infant skeleton hanging from its mother's tit.
As a poet I'm fixed in this page,
a white desire, backgrounded by Nestlé's saleswomen
disguised as nurses to sell Sahel mothers powdered milk,
a folly, as was even Black Elk
who even with his vision ligatious to his people
could do nothing for them against the lava
avalanche of gun power moving west.

I roll Wagadu across my students' faces, a die,
a four-fold city, a dream, and catch myself
passing on this tetrad as a symbol of human wholeness.
But isn't Wagadu just one more dream of a center,
an indestructable city of the mind dreamed up
from its actual absence? Yet within the mind
the friction against what goes on outside
is reconceiving the mountain, is painting it black
as a reaction against that child's hunger.
So the Wagadu I hand them is a skeletal four-fold dream,
a dream fom the Sahel maybe 2500 years old,
intact in "The Lute of Gassir,"
but once we look out the window
the text is a kind of die; what number would it turn up
if rolled by a bloated Sahel child?
Suppose we rolled it onto the table at a Nestlé's board meeting?
Art is only truthful
when seen in context—and its truth,
like its freedom, is to resist
the forming of autonomous centers,
centers that believe their existence is not contingent.
If I roll Wagadu into a Sahel maternity ward
there is a center for an instant, the power of its vision may
take a blow-torch to the powdered milk deception,
immediately another center is formed,
the mothers should leave that ward,

now what do they believe? The multinational corporation claims
powdered milk is better than mother milk.
Gassir's lute cries the Dausi, the song of its struggles,
will not die. What weak desire
cut the sky from the horizon, degraded gravity
and called it earth, what powerful weak desire
unmingled the ghosts from the living person,
then packed these severings into a void
around which it danced!
Within the flux—or is it the violence—of the grass,
the Dachau beetle appears—or is the Wagadu die
propelled by the argument for and against folds
that goes on in my own mind? Desire for indestructability
vies with phalanxes of bloated children,
I have a piece of die, or is it a rock that
from a certain angle looks like a die?
Caryl's face beams from the imaginary head I struggle with,
at the back of that head is the just opened door of Dachau,
on one side of the head another face appears,
an auroch from Lascaux—how I would like a wholeness
to be implied by the animal dimension of Caryl
versus human cruelty; should I bring in a fourth face
to fill this out? As I was staring at Wagadu
these three appeared and where a fourth might have been,
nothing but a blank wall,
a concrete block wall
a black political prisoner on Robben Island
watches this very evening, where for fifteen years
he has broken rocks with a hand-sledge . . .

and then white sailors began to appear
rushing every which way visoring their eyes
peering into the horizon, as if they had been ordered on deck
to know something there, and as I continued to dream
they formed ranks, diagonally passing through each other
always peering with their hands held to their brows
until there was only a loom of their motion, a machine of peering . . .

Upon waking I seemed to see what they had sought:
along the horizon a Canterbury of beautiful people were camped,
of all ages, all times, Hollywood pagans, actor priests,
with mirrors and cosmetics, entertaining and saving each other.

I seemed to hold some of that Robben Island prisoner's
anguish, perhaps a small part of it, but enough
to watch the meat turning in my hands,
to grasp, through adored white flesh,
the cinders of our conspiracy against our Siamese other.

Printed July 1978 in Santa Barbara & Ann Arbor
for the Black Sparrow Press by Mackintosh and Young
& Edwards Brothers Inc. Design by Barbara Martin.
This edition is published in paper wrappers; there
are 200 hardcover copies numbered & signed by the
author; & 26 lettered copies have have been handbound
in boards by Earle Gray each containing an original
holograph poem by the author.

Photo: Al Vandenberg

Clayton Eshleman was born June 1, 1935, in Indianapolis, Indiana. He began to write while attending Indiana University (1953-1961) where he received a BA in Philosophy and an MAT in Creative Writing and English Literature. Since then, he has traveled widely, living in Japan, Korea, Mexico, Peru and France. He has translated the poetry of Pablo Neruda, César Vallejo, Aimé Césaire and Antonin Artaud; in the spring of 1979 the University of California Press will publish "César Vallejo: The Complete Posthumous Poetry," translated by Eshleman and José Rubia Barcia. From 1967 through 1973, Eshleman published and edited *Caterpillar* magazine. He presently lives with his wife Caryl in west Los Angeles. From the fall of 1978 to the spring of 1979 he will be in south central France, continuing his research on the painted paleolithic caves, on a Guggenheim Fellowship.